Kordian

by
Juliusz Słowacki

translated, with notes and introduction by
Gerard T. Kapolka

GREEN LANTERN PRESS

Published by The Green Lantern Press, 2010
1511 N. Milwaukee Avenue, Second Floor
Chicago, Illinois 60622-2009
www.press.thegreenlantern.org

ISBN 978-1-4507-4208-5
First Edition of 500

Cover screenprinted in an edition of 500 by Aay Preston-Myint.

CONTENTS

Preface

Kordian is a difficult play to interpret, even for those who are well acquainted with Poland's history and literary traditions. It will be all the more difficult for English readers unfamiliar with that heritage. Like most other major works of Polish literature *Kordian* is intimately bound with questions of Polish history, Polish national consciousness, and the future of the Polish nation. Nevertheless, only a handful of other works from the canon of Polish literature could be said to be as crucial for the understanding of the development of Polish literature as a whole, the development of Poland's Romantic movement (her literary golden age), and certain self-critical aspects of the Polish national character. *Kordian* acts as a foil to Poland's national tragedy, *Forefathers' Eve Part III* by Adam Mickiewicz, and it is required reading in all Polish schools. Together with *Forefathers' Eve* and Zygmunt Krasiński's *Undivine Comedy*, *Kordian* forms a trilogy of Polish Messianism, which was pivotal to the Romantic age. It is also one of the most popular plays in Polish culture, in constant production somewhere in the country. An English translation of this play is long overdue.

I became acquainted with Juliusz Słowacki when I visited Poland to learn the language in 1974. Słowacki's imagery is unmistakably vivid. While there are many aspects of poetry that severely challenge the translator, the imagery, at least, can be rendered in English. Therefore, I feel that Słowacki may be one of the more accessible Polish poets for English readers. For too long the rich treasure trove of Polish literature has been almost inaccessible to an English speaking audience. In some ways, this is due to the Polonocentric nature of the best of the literature. But in these days, as the world gets smaller and we see how interconnected we all are, I feel that it is time to draw a bit more attention to the culture of Poland, a culture with which we are coming into greater contact. The concerns of the Polish nation to maintain its identity in the nineteenth century are, after all, not much different than the concerns of other groups and nations around the world right now. Poland's sufferings in the nineteenth century were not sustained in a vacuum, and the Poles have always felt themselves to be a part of Western and, now, World culture as a whole. Understanding Poland in the nineteenth century can help us understand its suffering in World War II, the Soviet era, and its rebellion in the Solidarity era that is at least in part responsible for the break up of the Soviet Union and the ability of Ukraine, Lithuania, and many other nations to regain their independence.

In my introduction I have tried to provide essential background information so that non-Polish readers will be able to understand the play, an overview of the play's complex structure, and a brief analysis of some of its major themes. I have left the explanation of the more specific allusions to the notes. I have relied heavily on the Biblioteka Narodowa edition of *Kordian*, seventh edition, edited by Mieczysław Inglot (Wrocław: 1986), especially for the information contained in its introduction and notes. This edition also provided the Polish text from which my translation was made.

Like most Polish verse, *Kordian* uses syllabic versification. The thirteen syllable line dominates, but eleven and eight syllable lines are also used. The text is rhymed throughout in various patterns, but seldom in couplets. In deference to Słowacki's obvious fondness for Shakespeare, I have rendered most of the play into (contemporary) blank verse. This seems to best suit the subject matter. I have, however, used rhymes in several sections where it seemed appropriate: the Motto; the Prologue; all scenes dominated by supernatural powers (including the entire "Preparation" section); the scene in which Kordian is confronted by the personified "Terror" and "Imagination"; the fable told in Act I; and all songs and verse that are sung or recited within the play. Here too I have continued the irregular iambic meter, sometimes shortening the lines.

For purposes of prosody, I must note how various names and places must be pronounced:

KORDIAN = Kor´ dyahn
TWARDOWSKI = Tvar dof´ skee
GRZEGORZ = Gzheh´ gosh (o as in English *for*)
JANEK = Yah´ neck
KAZIMIERZ = Kah zhee´ myesh
MACIEJOWICE = Mah chay o vee´ tseh
IVAN (Russian) = Ee vahn´
DĄBROWSKI = Dome brof´ skee

ii

Introduction

In 966 Poland received recognition as a sovereign state with roughly
its present boundaries. In 1385 a dynastic union with Lithuania,
which controlled much of what is now Belarus and Ukraine, joined
the fates of the two countries, which were formally unified in 1569
with the creation of the Commonwealth of Two Nations, a multi-
ethnic, multi-religious state that was one of the most powerful and
largest in Europe. In the seventeenth and eighteenth centuries, wars,
domestic chaos, rivalry among the magnates, and foreign influence
brought about a decline that eventually led to the three partitions, the
first in 1772 where Russia, Prussia, and Austria each bit off a chunk
of Poland. After a new constitution was passed by parliament May 3,
1791, Poland was invaded by Russia to prevent its implementation.
A group of Polish magnates, unhappy with the constitution, backed
the Russian invasion, and were eventually joined by the king himself,
Stanisław Augustus Poniatowski. Poniatowski had been instrumental
in the reform process that led to the constitution. This resulted in
a second partition of 1793 in which Russia and Prussia took part.
Tadeusz Kościuszko, a hero in the American Revolutionary War,
led an insurrection to secure Polish freedom. This insurrection has
captured the imagination of Polish patriots, largely because it was
a united effort of gentry, peasants, and Jews to free the Polish state
from foreign domination. In a legendary battle at Racławice, a group
of Polish peasants, armed only with scythes and led by Kosciuszko,
overran a Russian artillery position. Unfortunately, this insurrection
came to a bloody end under the leadership of the famed Russian
general Suvarov. This led to the final partition that erased Poland from
the map of Europe. The Poles later tried to hitch their hopes for the
resurrection of their state to Napoleon's star, and many Poles fought
for the Emperor in his campaigns. This led to the establishment of
the Duchy of Warsaw, a small fraction of the old Commonwealth,
but this too was destroyed with Napoleon. The Congress of Vienna,
at the end of the Napoleonic wars, established a Kingdom of Poland,
roughly coinciding with the Duchy of Warsaw, but smaller still, and
with the Czar of Russia as its king. The constitution of this kingdom
was considered the most liberal in Europe, but Czar Alexander
I abandoned his liberal ideals and turned despot after 1819 and

repeatedly crushed the constitution. His successor, Czar Nicholas I, even more despotic, would continue this policy.

The third act of *Kordian* is set in the twenty-four hours surrounding Czar Nicholas' coronation as King of Poland on May 24, 1829. Although the action of the play is entirely contrived, it is based on historical fact. There *was* a conspiracy to assassinate the Czar at the time of his coronation, spearheaded by Polish officer cadets. While that conspiracy came to nothing, and no actual attempt was made on the Czar's life, it was undoubtedly an important step in preparation for the later insurrection on November 29 of the following year. Once again, the 1830 insurrection was sparked by the enthusiasm of the cadets and junior officers to rid the country of Russia's domination. Meanwhile senior officers, pessimistic as to the outcome, joined the insurrection hesitantly or not at all. The romantic view of that insurrection claims that the enthusiasm of its youths was betrayed, at least in spirit, by older officers' resignation to defeat.

Juliusz Słowacki was born on August 4, 1809 in Krzemieniec, Volhynia. His father was Euzebiusz Słowacki, a poet and literature professor, first at the lyceum in Krzemieniec and later at the University of Wilno. His mother was Salomea née Januszewska. The graceful and sentimental Salomea exerted a strong influence on her slight, sickly, and willful son all of his life. Euzebiusz died early, when his only child was five years old. Salomea remarried another university professor, August Beçu, a medical doctor with strong musical talent. Together Salomea and August maintained one of the best salons in Wilno (Vilnius), patronizing both music and poetry. The early works of Adam Mickiewicz, published in that city when Juliusz was an adolescent, also found their way into the Beçu salon.

Although Słowacki, like Mickiewicz, came from the petty gentry, he was raised in an atmosphere of intellectual elitism. Also unlike Mickiewicz, Słowacki had no need to earn a living through his writings; he was supported by his family his whole short life. In addition to Polish literature, Słowacki was also well read in French and English, and the influence of the English Romantics and Shakespeare are particularly apparent in both his poetry and drama.

Like that of most romantic poets, Słowacki's life contained an unhappy first love, for Ludwika Śniadecka. She was older than the future poet and the daughter of an eminent professor of chemistry at the university. Another event that probably contributed to the future poet's pessimism was the suicide of his boyhood friend, Ludwik Spicnagel. Although we must be careful not to identify the hero Kordian too closely with Słowacki himself, it seems likely that Ludwik provides the inspiration for the suicide referred to in the opening lines of Act I, Scene 1 of the play, and that Ludwika is at least the partial inspiration for Laura.

After finishing a law degree at the University of Wilno, Słowacki went to Warsaw where he became a minor official in the Ministry of the Treasury. He was there when the November Insurrection broke out in 1830. Although Słowacki demonstrated his solidarity with the Insurrectionists in his verse, he did not take active part in the fighting, mostly because of his ill health, and his mother's concern for his safety. He did, however, act as an envoy for the insurgent government and journeyed to Paris to call for help from the West. After the failure of his mission, Słowacki inevitably joined the so-called "Great Emigration" of the leaders of the Insurrection who were forced into exile. That group included many artists and intellectuals, and Paris became the cultural capital of Poland for the next few decades. Słowacki always felt guilty for not taking an active part in the fighting and for leaving his country while the fighting was going on.

Kordian was the last to be published of three plays written in quick succession after the failure of the November Insurrection by three different poet/playwrights who, largely because of those works, are often regarded as the three great bards of Poland. A great irony of Polish literature is that even though each play was inspired by the November Insurrection, not one is actually about the event itself.

The second play, Zygmunt Krasiński's *Undivine Comedy* (1833), although a masterpiece in its own right, exerted little or no influence on *Kordian*. For our purposes it is thus not discussed here. In order to contextualize Słowacki's play, however, I must say something about the first play.

The first, and by almost all accounts the greatest, was *Forefather's Eve, Part III (Dziady)* by Adam Mickiewicz. Mickiewicz had already achieved the status of Poland's greatest poet before the publication of this masterpiece and his later (1834) *Pan Tadeusz*. In 1823 he had published *Forefather's Eve, Parts II and IV* while still in Wilno. Part II presents a stylized version of the pagan Lithuanian festival to which the title of the play refers. According to tradition, Forefather's

Eve is a night when the spirits of one's ancestors (or others) may be summoned. There were several such days on the calendar before the advent of Christianity, but it was later usually celebrated on Halloween. Part IV presents the character Gustaw, or his ghost, visiting a hermit and relating his tale of star-crossed love.

Shortly after the publication of this play, Mickiewicz was arrested for his participation in the Philomaths, which served as a front for several conspiratorial groups. It was his arrest and exile that became the subject matter for *Forefathers' Eve, Part III*, published in 1832. At the beginning of this play, the hero writes on his cell wall that Gustaw died November 1, 1823 and Konrad was born on the same day. The name "Konrad" refers to another of Mickiewicz's triumphs, *Konrad Wallenrod*, a romantic epic published in 1828 while Mickiewicz was in Russia. *Konrad Wallenrod* is about the grand master of the Teutonic Knights who, according to this epic, became aware of his Lithuanian ancestry and purposely led the militant monastic order to ruin. The main character's name change, from Gustaw to Konrad, therefore, reveals a maturation of Polish Romanticism, from its preoccupation with self-indulgent love, to a preoccupation with the national question. Konrad instantly became the epitome of the suffering hero, a kind of Christ figure who would redeem his country through his suffering. Konrad's close association, even identification, with Mickiewicz himself, may seem like supreme hubris to us, but it was in keeping with the Romantic view of the poet. At the play's most famous moment, Konrad falls just short of the blasphemy of accusing God of being a Czar.

Forefather's Eve, Part III immediately became an icon of Polish Messianism, a popular movement within Romanticism, especially among the Paris emigrés, whose "guru" was Andrzej Towiański.

Both Mickiewicz and Słowacki were at one time disciples of Towiański, but Słowacki later rejected him and embraced his own form of Messianism. Simply put, Polish Messianism held that Poland was the Christ of Nations. She had suffered and died, but she would be resurrected. Her resurrection would result in the salvation of all of Europe. Mickiewicz saw himself as the spokesman for the nation as its national poet, yet he also saw himself suffering for untold others in other countries. This explains why the relatively minor incident in Wilno, in which a few young men were arrested and exiled could be treated as more significant than the defeat of thousands in the

Kordian

November Insurrection. Nevertheless, this view was not shared by all. It was certainly not held by Słowacki.

That *Kordian* (published in 1834) is meant as an answer to *Forefathers' Eve, Part III* can be seen in the title itself. "Kordian" is an anagram of "Konrad," the hero of Mickiewicz's play (the extraneous "i" is necessary for the pronunciation in Polish, "Kordan" would be untenable). Słowacki was about ten years younger than Mickiewicz, and by the time he came onto the literary scene, Mickiewicz had already achieved his reputation as national bard. Rivalry with Mickiewicz seems to have been a kind of obsession for Słowacki, but we should remember that some of the first salvos in this rivalry were fired by Mickiewicz, who called Słowacki's early verses "a pretty church in which there is no God." Furthermore, an especially painful insult is contained in *Forefather's Eve, Part III*: a character named "the Doctor" and representing Bęcu, Słowacki's stepfather, is struck down by lightning as punishment for his collaboration with Novosiltsov, the Czar's henchman in Wilno.

Knowing that *Kordian* is an answer to *Forefathers' Eve, Part III* does not provide all the answers to questions about how to interpret Kordian the character and Słowacki's relationship to him. Two possibilities stand out, and both are probably valid up to a point. One is that Kordian represents the active hero in contrast to Konrad's passive, suffering hero. The extant play, *Kordian*, is the first part of an intended trilogy that Słowacki never completed. A few fragments remain which indicate that the poet's intentions were to concentrate on the November Insurrection in the second play and its aftermath in the third. This is also implied in the "Preparations" section in the extant work. Słowacki clearly resented Mickiewicz's pretensions to being the national savior when he was not even present in Poland during this important uprising. Kordian's attempt to actively influence history by assassinating the Czar is thus set in contrast to Konrad's passive suffering for the nation.

The problem with viewing Kordian as an active hero, however, is that he blatantly fails in his attempt at action. We do not know if he is meant to redeem himself in the following plays of the trilogy. Assuming that his character remains consistent and will not redeem himself, we arrive at a second possible interpretation for the ultimate significance of the anagram, i.e. that Kordian is meant to represent a character very much like Konrad and not his foil. The implication here is that the Romantic sensitivities are fine for a "suffering hero" but lead to paralysis when action is called for. If we were to place Konrad into a situation like the November Uprising, what might result is a lot of Romantic posturing without any tangible results. In this way Kordian becomes an indictment not just against Mickiewicz, but against the entire Romantic movement, and ironically against Słowacki himself.

Events in *Kordian's* third act are not autobiographical, but in many ways Kordian is an autobiographical character. His preoccupations and sensibilities reflect Słowacki's, and his attempts at action seem to mirror Słowacki's own desire. The ineffectiveness of Kordian's actions may be a projection of what Słowacki might have faced had he joined the fighting of the insurrection. In any event the pessimism and ambivalence toward Romantic sensibilities is typical of Słowacki as well as later European Romanticism. That pessimism stands in sharp contrast to Mickiewicz.

A key motif in the polemic with Mickiewicz on the subject of Polish Messianism is the allusion to the Swiss national hero, Arnold Winkelried, who barred the narrow mountain road to the Austrian forces by offering his own body to the spears of the enemy. Calling Poland "The Winkelried of Nations" as Kordian does at the end of Act II, opposes the view of Mickiewicz and many of the other emigrés that Poland, as the "Christ of Nations," will rise again triumphant after its period of suffering. Słowacki's view is much more pessimistic: that the sacrifice of the nation must be selfless, that resurrection cannot be expected. This allegory, that Poland is the "Winkelried of Nations," is idiosyncratic to Słowacki, an idea derived from his stay in Switzerland, where *Kordian* was written. It is, however, connected to a much older concept of Poland as the *antemurale* (bulwark) of Christianity. This term derives from the centuries of European struggle with the Turks, but its implication is most significant. As the bulwark, Poland will be the first to fall, but its falling buys time and gives a warning to the rest of Europe. A more contemporary image would be that of a "point man" on an infantry patrol.

Through all of this, Słowacki's attack on Mickiewicz in this play remains ideological and does not descend to the personal. (Future works by Słowacki will not always be so restrained.) It thus warrants our attention all the more. *Kordian* is almost a necessary companion

piece to *Forefathers' Eve, Part III*; it rounds out the image of Polish
Romanticism generally, and Polish Messianism in particular.
Kordian begins a current of self-critical national reflection that will
be taken up by historians and other artists in ensuing decades. It
also demonstrates Słowacki's strong social democratic tendencies
in calling for action from the crowd in the third act. However, in
this it is the precedent for another trend in both Polish literature
and, unfortunately, Polish history: the gulf that exists between the
crowd and the intellectual leadership, and the mistrust and lack of
cooperation that results from it. Kordian attempts to act alone when
the conspiracy rejects the assassination of the Czar and his family.
The gulf between the people and the intelligentsia is a theme later
explored more specifically in Stanisław Wyspiański's *Wesele* (The
Wedding). It manifested itself in history as recently as 1968 when the
people refused to support the intellectuals in their rebellion, and in
1970 when the intellectuals failed to support the people. "Solidarity"
and more recent political events, including the freeing of the Polish
state from Soviet domination, may have lessened this age-old stigma,
but scars undoubtedly remain.

Despite the obvious technical difficulties that staging *Kordian*
presents, Słowacki did seem to write it for the stage and not as a
"closet drama." The emphasis on "buskins" (the elevated shoes worn
by Greek actors) by the Third Person of the Prologue, whose speech
we will discuss below, seems to make this clear. This is another way
in which it differs polemically from Mickiewicz's work. In his travels,
Słowacki was fascinated by the brilliant theatrical effects being
achieved on the stage in Paris and elsewhere in Europe. The elaborate
settings of *Kordian* were meant to be staged in the same way, although
we do not know if, considering the state of the Polish nation, he
expected his play to actually receive such a production.

Słowacki had probably intended to create a masterpiece in
Kordian to rival and outshine *Forefathers' Eve, Part III*. Few among
Polish literary historians would quite grant him this judgment. Still,
Kordian is both a masterpiece in its own right and Słowacki's first real
dramatic success. He would go on to create a broad range of dramas
on Polish themes.

Kordian

As a dramatist, Słowacki had many influences, foremost among them probably Shakespeare, Hugo, and Calderón, who wrote for the stage, as well as the closet dramatists Goethe and Shelley. Polish Enlightenment drama had reached a high point in Słowacki's lifetime through the comedies of Aleksander Fredro. Słowacki was able to combine his Romantic sensibilities, his genius for imagery, and the techniques he borrowed from the masters mentioned above with Fredro's theatricality. He thus achieved a synthesis in a wide range of dramas which had a huge influence on the rich history of subsequent Polish drama. Słowacki's dramatic output leads eventually to the great symbolist drama of Stanisław Wyspiański and the innovative dramas of Stanisław Ignacy Witkiewicz and Witold Gombrowicz.

A frequent complaint about *Kordian* is its complex and seemingly disorganized structure. Most commentators divide it into six parts, the short motto, the "Preparations," the Prologue, and each of the three acts. Even if we dismiss the motto and the Prologue from the action of the play proper, we are left with four dramatic segments, each written in a radically different style, whose thematic links are, at best, subtle. Such innovative dramatic license confounds even those of us who have had a heavy dose of twentieth century dramatic innovations. They must have been considered chaotic by most of Słowacki's contemporaries. Yet each of these sections serves a purpose. The radically different styles of the three acts of the play reflect, among other things, the maturation of Kordian as hero and poet. The first act deals with Kordian's love for the unattainable Laura and ends in his attempted suicide, an incident which might be seen to echo Goethe's *Sorrows of Young Werther*. The second act, with its constant changes of setting, could represent Kordian's searching for a kind of purpose in life, with each scenario rejected until he decides, after climbing Mont Blanc, to take Winkelried as his model. In the third act we see him putting that plan into action

Even though there is a great deal of evidence that Słowacki did conceive of *Kordian* as a drama for the stage, the inclusion of the "motto" and its importance to the play indicates Słowacki's sense that *Kordian* would first be read as a "closet" drama. The motto sets the stage for the trilogy as a whole, not just the first play. It is a fragment of Słowacki's poetic novel, *Lambro* (1832), which is set during the Greek war for independence against the Turks. The dominant image in the fragment, a dead man's heart wrapped in an aloe leaf, is connected to the title of our drama. "Kordian" is not only an anagram from "Konrad," it is also derived from the Latin, *cor, cordis,* heart. The heart, wrapped in an aloe leaf on which are written words of resurrection, will never come back to life, yet its preservation still provides a "secret": a spark is retained in this heart, which the poet will attempt to stir into a blaze. Herein lies a foreshadowing of Słowacki's attitude toward Messianism as Mickiewicz represents it. By using this fragment as a motto for a very Polish play while also drawing on the ancient and exotic culture of Egypt, Słowacki universalizes the plight of Poland. This is totally in keeping with the concept of Polish Messianism.

The "Preparation" section of the play also warrants special attention. These are the "preparations" for the nineteenth century, consisting primarily of Satan and his subordinate devils creating actors for the next century, concentrating specifically on Poland. Słowacki's influences in creating this scene are many, but *Macbeth* and *Faust* predominate. This scene comes before the action of the play proper and before the Prologue. It is a kind of introduction to the entire trilogy. In many ways it reflects some of the elements in *Forefathers' Eve, Part III* and, like the supernatural elements of that play, serves the purpose of placing the action of the play (or trilogy) on a higher plane, giving it greater significance than mere earthly suffering and action. But, unlike Mickiewicz, Słowacki treats his devils with considerable humor. This demonstrates a certain parodic intent in the play.

The "Preparation" is an important section that introduces several themes. First of all, it provides the element of *ananke* (necessity), which the Romantics believed to be essential to tragedy. It reminds us both of the witches in Shakespeare's *Macbeth* and the Prologue in Heaven to Goethe's *Faust*. Satan, here, is introduced reminiscing about Twardowski, Poland's own Faust character who makes a deal with the devil. Thus Satan is here a particularly Polish devil. This is the "preparation" for the nineteenth century, but more specifically, it is the preparation for the November Insurrection, and the ensuing defeat. To prepare for the defeat, the devils are shown creating functionaries for Poland. These functionaries, who represent specific historical personages (identified later in the notes to that section), introduce the theme of old men stifling the enthusiasm of the young instigators of the insurrection. When Satan first turns his attention to Poland, he talks of the knights whose swords "are bent/ Like the devil's horns, like the lunar crescent./ No sign of the cross on the saber's hilt." This reference to the traditional sword of the Polish gentry conjures up images of the Sarmatian republic, with its "golden freedom" and *liberum veto* and the anarchy that they produced, which many later historians will blame for the fall of the Polish Commonwealth.

Kordian is a metaphysical as well as a political drama. A major, pervasive theme is introduced here which is central to the development of Romanticism as a whole. The devils, with their grotesque clock of history and their identification with "rapacious nature," in many ways represent (or parody) the Enlightenment cosmology. The Deists of the Enlightenment saw the universe as a kind of giant clock, which God once made but abandoned to tick on its own. A major impetus of the Romantic movement was a revolt against this concept which leaves the individual as nothing more than a cog in a machine. As a Romantic, Słowacki sees such a mechanical universe as demonic rather than divine. By presenting the force of nature as evil rather than good, (as would such Romantics as Wordsworth), or neutral, (as would modern scientists), Słowacki anticipates the Manichean stance that Czesław Miłosz would later espouse in such works as *Native Realm* and *The Land of Ulro*.

xiv

When Kordian comes onto the scene, we realize that like most Romantics, Słowacki rejects the scientific viewpoint of the world. Yet he also places little hope in God or other supernatural forces. Thus *Kordian* is not only a good example of the later, pessimistic trend in Romanticism, but also an important precursor to literary modernism. Like the modernists, Słowacki turns to allusion and literary formalism to impose an order on the chaos of the universe. This is represented by the "Third Person of the Prologue" who thus synthesizes the "spiritual" First Person with the pragmatic (empirical) Second Person.

An important dichotomy, which becomes a strong motif in the play, is presented at the end of the "Preparation" section. When the angels chase the devils away, the Archangel recounts his tale of brushing against the earth and, without being specific, also recounts the tale of Poland's suffering. He asks God that more blood than tears should flow, which we should interpret as a call to action rather than suffering to bring about the salvation of the nation. It places the Archangel (generally accepted to be the Archangel Michael) on the side of the Insurrectionists, even though he knows that the Insurrection will end in failure, and against the suffering Messianism of Mickiewicz.

The Prologue presents three "Persons" who can be interpreted in terms of rudimentary Hegelianism (popular among Romantics, including Słowacki) to form a thesis, antithesis, and synthesis. The First Person of the Prologue clearly represents Mickiewicz, and by extension, all like-minded poets and Messianists, who support Mickiewicz's ideal of the suffering nation and her suffering spokesman. The apocalyptic imagery and grandiose poetry of the First Person mimics the style of "The Great Improvisation" section of *Forefathers' Eve*. The speech of the Second Person of the Prologue is simply an attack on that of the First. It is a kind of demystification of the first's speech, and presents him, after all, as only a man. Although this speech is entirely negative in character, it is taken by some critics to represent the standpoint of the social democrats, who called for action instead of poetic pretense. The Third Person of the Prologue synthesizes poetry and action through drama. He makes specific references to the stage, and as such, he might represent the producer, and certainly Słowacki himself, the playwright. The play will capture and preserve the spirits of the dead knights, just as the aloe leaf of the motto preserves the heart.

After these three introductory sections, the first play of the trilogy properly begins. Still, there is little formal unity among *Kordian's* three acts. The first act presents the young lover, one equally preoccupied with the reason for his own existence as he is with love. There are strong allusions to *Hamlet* throughout this act as Kordian tries to decide whether to kill himself or take an active role in the world. Two important influences on his life are presented. Laura— whose archetypical name reinforces her role—is treated by Kordian much the same way that Hamlet treats Ophelia, but with less tragic results. Indications are that Laura treats Kordian more like a son than a lover. This would seem to justify our seeing Kordian's love for Laura as reflective of Słowacki's for the older Ludwika Śniadecka. The love interest of Kordian also runs parallel to *Forefathers' Eve Part IV*, in which Gustaw (or his ghost) tells his tale of woe to the Hermit.[1]

The other influence on Kordian is Grzegorz, the faithful old servant. He is a former legionnaire, and his two tales of his war experiences show that he was with Napoleon in 1798 and in 1812, making him a model of the faithful soldier. He tells three tales to Kordian meant to instruct him in this critical period. The first is a fable about a young man who gains his fortune by making shoes for dogs. This light tale is a superb example of the way in which Słowacki can use comedy to make quite serious points, for the moral of the story is that a will to victory is everything. This is reinforced by the story of Napoleon in Egypt. The third story, about the defeat in 1812 and the heroic action of Kazimierz, the young officer, is an important foreshadowing of the Winkelried theme. The young officer dies in a futile attempt to save the old soldiers and while his surname has been forgotten his action never will be.

The second act, entitled "The Year 1828: The Wanderer" is both innovative and jarring. Even though it is set in five radically different locations, it is not divided into scenes. At times symbolist, surreal, and absurd, variant actions and settings flow swiftly from one to another. The wanderings of Kordian could represent the Grand Tour that young European gentlemen are expected to make. It also seems to prefigure the period after the 1830 insurrection, often called "The Great Emigration," in which many Polish patriots were forced to wander the West in exile. The title of the act works against such an interpretation, but there are several seeming anachronisms in Act II.

The second act has little to do with historical facts and more to do with the development of the hero. Each of the segments resolves an aspect of the uncertainties Kordian expressed in the first act.

---

1. The reader unfamiliar with Polish literature will be, at this time, quite confused about the numbering of the "Parts" of *Forefathers' Eve*. Mickiewicz published Parts II and IV in Wilno in 1823. An embryonic Part I exists, but it was not published at that time. It is not known what Mickiewicz meant by then omitting Part III. When he wrote Part III (published in Dresden, 1832), he begins it by having the main character change his name from Gustaw to Konrad in the way described. Since Part IV presents Gustaw, as a ghost, telling his tale to the hermit, it does come logically after the events of his life, as far as the chronology of the play goes. Part III, however, represents a later development in the history of Mickiewicz's Romantic ideas, and it thus comes later in another sense. Since Słowacki had decided to let his character survive his suicide attempt, he has no need for such convolutions.

Kordian

Continuing the *Hamlet* allusion, the wanderings of Kordian serve the
same purpose as Hamlet's trip toward England with Rosencrantz and
Guildenstern. Hamlet returns resolved, especially after contemplating
the actions of Fortinbras. The resolution of Kordian's dilemmas come
in the form of the bursting of several Romantic bubbles. In St. James
Park, Kordian is brought down from his Wordsworthean idyll by the
pragmatic chair attendant. At Dover, his metaphysical contemplation
of the abyss is humbled by his contemplation of the passage from
King Lear (which, not incidentally, is a tremendous example of old
age not conferring wisdom, reinforcing the theme introduced in the
"Preparation" section). In Italy, with Violetta, the bubble of Romantic
love is burst. Finally, in his audience with the Pope, Kordian loses all
hope of the Roman Catholic Church supporting the cause of Poland
when the Pope rejects his sacred relic of the ashes of the victims of
the Praga massacre of 1794. This also represents a crisis of faith for
Kordian. And so, when Kordian sits atop Mount Blanc at the end of
the act and once again turns to metaphysical speculation, he has been
stripped of all his delusions. The only thing that remains is a totally
selfless sacrifice. Not a Christ-like sacrifice leading to resurrection
and reverence, but a sacrifice with no hope of resurrection, like that
of Winkelried, or that of Kazimierz from Grzegorz's tale. The third
act is a self-contained drama, which even obeys the classical unities of
time and action. It presents the Coronation Conspiracy proper. The
action returns to something resembling standard drama, but there are
still outstanding innovations: crowd scenes where an entire square in
Warsaw must be presented onstage, the coronation scene consisting
of a single word (two words in the translation: "I swear"), but which
conveys considerable meaning, the use of mental states as characters
when Kordian hesitates before attempting to assassinate the Czar, and
an appearance of Satan in the guise of a modern doctor attempting
to take over Kordian's soul (just as the devil attempted to take over
Konrad's in Mickiewicz's play). All of this, of course, is combined with
Słowacki's marvelous, forceful imagery.

Yet another strong allusion to Shakespeare is introduced in this
act: an allusion to the assassination of Julius Caesar. But here, the
situation is reversed. Instead of a reluctant Brutus being brought into
a group of convinced conspirators, we are presented with a convinced
Kordian, trying to persuade a reluctant group of conspirators. But the
Romantics are not ancient Romans, and Kordian remains closer to

Hamlet than Brutus in the end.

All of his creative life, Słowacki was obsessed with his rivalry for Mickiewicz. History has continued to refuse Słowacki quite the stature of his rival, but perhaps this is like comparing apples and oranges. Mickiewicz's work is like the seemingly effortless creations of classical Greek sculptors or the masters of the Renaissance. Słowacki's works are vibrant with virtuosity and strong emotion like the statues of the Hellenistic period or the violent emotions of the Baroque.

Though Słowacki may have failed in his attempt to topple Mickiewicz as the national bard, his efforts have certainly won him a permanent place in the Canon of Polish literature. *Kordian* itself is one of Słowacki's masterpieces, and it is regularly produced on the Polish stage, as are many of Słowacki's subsequent dramas. I hope that this translation, with its notes and introduction, will help to make this masterpiece accessible to those who do not have the ability to experience it in its original language.

Juliusz Słowacki

Kordian

**First part of the trilogy *The Coronation Conspiracy*,
translated from the Polish by
Gerard T. Kapolka**

At the edge I'll sing to the world beyond;
I'll stir the fire to find a spark.
Egyptians used an aloe frond
To wrap the dead man's withered heart;
The leaf holds words of resurrection;
And still the heart comes not to life,
Yet here the heart has gained protection
Lest it turn to dust... The hour strikes
When thought must solve the secret riddle!
The answer's in the heart—in the middle.

Juliusz Słowacki, *Lambro*[2]

---

2. This "Motto" is an excerpt from Canto I of Słowacki's poetic novel, *Lambro*
(vv. 124–133). These verses are sung by the hero, a Greek National bard, in trying to
gather his countrymen to fight against the Turks.

The Preparation[3]

The Night of December 31, 1799. The hut of the famous sorcerer, Twardowski,[4] in the Carpathian Mountains. In front of the hut a spacious courtyard, rocks further on. Below leafless beech woods. The darkness is penetrated by flashes of lightning. A WITCH is combing her hair, singing...

WITCH
From the stars in the air
As I comb out my hair
Sparks crackle and fall
As from bright Polish swords;
Seen by Satan's dark hordes,
Who answer the call:
Lightning flares in the sky.
Feathers shriek as they fly;
And bend down the beech.

I

    SATAN flies down in the guise of a beautiful angel

SATAN
Well, has the hour now struck, my faithful witch?

WITCH
What hour?

SATAN
       The hour no man will hear
Strike twice in his life...

---

3. The "preparation" for the nineteenth century. This can also be read, however, as the preparation for the November Insurrection and its ultimate defeat.
4. Twardowski is the Polish "Faust," and his story runs parallel to the German legend, although the Polish tale is usually told with more humor. There are several variants, but they generally end with Twardwoski escaping the devil by seeking refuge on the moon.

Kordian

WITCH

That hour is near.
Before the eye can blink ten times
Atop the tow'r of Babel.
And though I were deaf, I'd hear the chimes.
But where's your fiendish rabble?
They make slow haste from heaven's dome;
The tortoise from which they fashioned my comb
Moved more quickly.

SATAN

Show that comb to me!
Tears well in my eyes... It was Twardowski's!
When I wore a dog's skin;[5] he combed my coat
As I fawned at his feet. Go out now, go!
The guests have been invited to the revels;
Here on Bald Mountain.[6]

Exit WITCH

SATAN *crying out*

To me, Devils!

Ten flashes of lightning and ten thousand devils descend

The sky rains devils, let them flood the ground!
If the trees of Eden are still around,[7]
Then man will gather bitter fruit in fall...
Sit down! I don't see you all.
Where is Mephistopheles?[8]

ASHTORETH[9]

He left, My Lord, if you please,
He flew down to the grave to say a prayer
For his old friend, Twardowski, the sooth-sayer.

---

5. According to folk tradition, the devil can appear in the form of a black dog.
6. Scene of the "Witches' Sabbath," cf. Moussorgsky's "Night on Bald Mountain."
7. The "Tree of Knowledge" from Genesis.
8. The devil made famous by Marlowe and Goethe in their Faust dramas.
9. A name for the devil, but originally a Syrian Moon Goddess and probably derived from the Phoenician goddess of love, Astarte.

Kordian

SATAN

He's taken on that style, devout and warm:
A poet's stance...[10] The moon now shows its horns—[11]
It's time to get to work...

DEVILS

What's your command?

SATAN

The clock of eternity! Watch each hand.
Use children's blood to grease the springs and gears,
To clearly sound the hours, the days, the years.
Bring it here! Set it up! Is it still whole?

ASHTORETH

The rust of ages takes no toll
On wheels and wires within this thing;
The clock face is a Host harangued
By the Leviathan's sharp fangs,[12]
The hours are shown by hornet's sting,
A dragon's tooth points out the day;
An endless strand of Satan's locks
Is wound throughout this dreaded clock.
Remember when that hair turned gray
With fright when he heard the thunder?... [13]
The mainspring, from the land of Tell
And Calvin,[14] is positioned well
Upon a human eye; no wonder
That it wears as well as gemstone.

---

10. A stab at Mickiewicz and his émigré circle, who had taken a religious stance.
11. The time of the New Moon and immediately afterwards, when the devil's work was said to be done.
12. Biblical beast, sometimes identified with the crocodile (as here), also sometimes associated with the whale (as in Melville's *Moby Dick*).
13. A reference to the rebellious angels being driven from heaven.
14. "The land of Tell / and Calvin," i.e. Switzerland. *Kordian* was written in Switzerland, and Swiss legends play a large role. William Tell, of course, is the Swiss hero who refused to doff his hat to the Austrian governor and was forced to shoot an apple off his son's head. John Calvin is the austere religious reformer. The Swiss, then as now, were famous for watchmaking, and frequently used jewels in their movements.

Kordian

Just hear the souls of sinners groan,
Amid the tangled springs and wheels
With every note of the chimes' peals...
The legs of a tarantula
Swing back and forth like pendula,
To drive the gears.

SATAN
                    Enough of this!
Gehenna, Ashtoreth, tenants of Dis,[15]
Be like accountants, the clock will soon chime!
Count days, the years, the centuries.

The clock strikes and the devils begin counting

                    Oh, World!
The serpent of eternity[16] has furled
Itself around you, in coils all entwined;
It strikes and bites you there and here;
Its fangs poison the centuries;
The ashes of dead memories
Have been scattered on your earth.
I was present at your birth.
A handful of earth in putrid atmosphere.
This corpse of chaos with a coffin of sky
Etched by the corrosion of time,
Mineral rust and granite bones,
With moss of flowers and forests o'ergrown,
As worms crawl around in your womb, they think
And scheme.
Woe to them if they don't limit their dreams
To Earth! Woe to them if they cross the brink!

GEHENNA
The nineteenth century strikes!

4

---

15. Gehenna is here used as a name for a devil but is derived from a Hebrew name for Hell. Dis was another name for Pluto, Roman God of the underworld, but it is also used for his domain.
16. The serpent devouring its own tail feeds on itself and forms a circle, symbolizing eternity.

Kordian

SATAN
                                        Count the years,
Ashtoreth! Perhaps the one that now shies
Thunderbolts from that cloud will try
To help some nation on the earth. I fear
That he has shortened this century.
Would he dare steal an hour from the Devil?
I won't be driven into penury!
Or I will once again turn rebel.
Almighty God must do me justice.
Nor will rapacious nature stand for this.[17]

ASHTORETH
The year Eighteen Hundred sounds!

SATAN
The wheel of torture is turning round?
Each tooth is ripping, each screw is tight'ning.
Soon the sky will flash with lightning,
The flashes last longer than these years,
When suff'ring drives this world to tears;
And every year glides idly as a snail
For silly, wretched, lovers of false hope;
And man crawls through the silv'ry slime, to grope
For scattered memories along its trail.
And sailors lost in the past
Have become historians;

5

---

17. Serious philosophical considerations lurk behind the surface humor of
Satan's speech both here and later when he assumes the form of The Doctor.
The philosophers of the Enlightenment, such as Voltaire and Rousseau, who
are mentioned later, tended to see the world as a kind of machine or clock,
which God may have made, but which forever runs its course without Divine
intervention (Deism, if God is posited). The Romantics rejected this conception
programmatically. Although those Enlightenment philosophers, especially
Rousseau, would have seen this machine, and the ticking away of Nature, as good,
here it is presented as evil, causing death, destruction, etc. The possibility of Divine
intervention is suggested by the year hiding behind the cloud. It will be strengthened
at the end of the section when the angels appear.

And writing calendars is now their task,[18]
With names of kings, and dates, and inscriptions.
Some tried thinking about thinking;
Philosophers thought hard on this,
Until they hung out o'er the brink
And woke up to see the abyss;
They shout, "It's dark! It's dark! We cannot see!"
That's a Hosanna for us devils,
An anthem straight out of our hymnals
He who thinks for an hour will be with me.
It's a devil's delight beyond compare!

Enter MEPHISTOPHELES

MEPHISTOPHELES
Your prophesies are a wondrous show,
Your cloak is patched with the works of Voltaire,
Your turban holds the goose quill of Rousseau.

6

SATAN
Mephistopheles, it's time for action,
Choose a plaything from the earthly hordes
German doctors give no satisfaction,
Manfreds wander on the Alps no more?
Monks no longer fast away in cells:[19]
So why don't you lead some soldier astray!

---

18. The calendars referred to were popular in the Baroque era and contained a
collection of useful and useless facts. They were similar to almanacs or encyclopediae.
In fact, this is precisely an attack on the French Encyclopedists and like-minded
Enlightenment philosophers. Louis Bonald, one of the Romantic opponents to the
Enlightenment, stated that those who would be guided in human affairs solely by
historical facts and experience, ignoring basic principles, were like sailors setting out
without a compass, using only accounts of previous voyages and ships' logs. (Louis
Bonald, *Pensées* in *Oeuvres completes*, Paris: 1864, vol. III, p. 1303; cited in Juliusz
Słowacki, *Kordian*, seventh edition, prepared by Mieczysław Inglot. Wrocław:
Biblioteka Narodowa, 1986, p. 9, notes.)
19. An allusion to *The Monk*, a gothic novel by Matthew Lewis (1775); the previous
lines refers to *Faust* and Byron's *Manfred*.

Kordian

MEPHISTOPHELES

Hell!

A soldier is a fish that shuns the seine,
His lamp is common sense, and with its light
He can avoid our cloven-hooved temptations.

SATAN

The only ones eluding us are knights?
Listen! Among the many nations,
There's one where blood will soon be spilt.
Go there! The knights carry swords that are bent
Like the devils' horns, like the lunar crescent.
No sign of the Cross on the saber's hilt.[20]
Help them—they will begin a battle soon,[21]
As we once waged on Him, the Lord of Hosts;
They'll pray, then kill, then curse, then boast—
They're nestled on their fathers' tombs,
With vengeance visions in their dreams.
The nation rose, was conquered, then was naught;
They shattered swords on hated enemies,
Who turned and killed them with a thought;
This thought possessed a mighty fist
Which used the thought like rope to twist
It round their necks, bound to a pillory
For folks to spit in their direction.

MEPHISTOPHELES

Just let me search my devils' psaltery
To find a psalm for resurrection;
I'll sing it for them, if I find the page.
This century, today, we have the right
Of making kings and beggars for this age.
Let's fashion dignitaries for these knights,
So we can cram the posts of government.
—The nation will be bound together

---

20. The reference is to Polish swords, which were curved and traditionally did not
bear a hilt in the form of a cross, as did most other swords.
21. The November Insurrection of 1830.

Into a book of old tooled leather,
And when their pow'r starts to ferment,
Their parchment brows will crackle.[22]

SATAN
Good advice. Let's form a circle.
We'll make men for this government!
Call the witches! Bring them here!

SATAN gives orders while the devils set to work

I gather all the elements
That lie beneath the crystal sphere
Of heaven, in continuum;
But separated by the chemists—
Put in this cauldron: platinum,
Carbon, oxygen... Blow, you spirits!
Thunder roars in the cauldron
Into the elements of earth
You must now throw the Corporal's pins[23]
With lacquered heads, which gave the birth
To plans of overthrowing kings—
They number forty thousand,
So throw them in the cauldron!

DEVILS
And?

SATAN
      And nothing.

DEVILS
                  What of his intelligence?

SATAN
What of it?

DEVILS
            Done.

---

22. The first instance of a motif that will be repeated throughout the play, that the elder statesmen and military leaders will betray the enthusiasm of the younger generation.
23. Napoleon ("the Corporal") used lacquered pins on a map to plan his battles.

8

Kordian

SATAN

Then let him fly!

The roar of thunder, a spirit flies out of the cauldron

An old grandfather passes by,
He does not fight, he does not toil;
But we will mock him with a name
That's inconsistent with his fame;[24]
He's joined to children of the soil
Because he bears the name of peasant!
Descend, now, from the vault of heaven,
Go down to these wretches! Rule!

DEVILS

Sire, is that all? Just one old fool?

SATAN

No, throw a diamond in the drink!
The diamond will be drowned in fire;
Now add the confidential ink
Used in the pen of Talleyrand,
The ink grows pale, the marks expire
Before the gaze of common sense.
Blow on the boiling cauldron, then
Perhaps we'll see what we command.

DEVILS

It's ready! But despite our plans,
We have produced a worthy man;
It seems the water in the kettle
Has grown too cold, been stirred too little.

SATAN

No loss—we'll use him all the more;
We'll set him up before the poor,
So they can kneel and beg his trust;
His face is like a Roman bust,

---

24. General Józef Chłopicki (1771–1854). His surname is derived from the word
chłop (peasant). He was the leader of the first stage of the Insurrection and was of
conservative bent.

As pictured on their coinage.
In order to put him to shame,
We will give him the devil's name,[25]
To contradict his lineage.
Now let him out! Now let him fly!

DEVILS

Well, better luck on the third try.

SATAN

Go now to the sign of Cancer,
Break off his brittle eyes and legs,
Then take the spurs off of a rooster
And throw them down into the dregs.
Next we will catch a timid snail,
And throw his horns into the pail.
What's in the kettle now?

DEVILS

          A knight.

SATAN

A leader! Walking like a crab,
And using horns, like snails, for sight.
When he touches anything, he hides
His horns within his shell. He grabs
The plans, and stashes them inside
The vault awaiting the cock crow.[26]
Take a list of rhymes and throw
It in this Polish kettle,
Add a million printer's marks,
And three poppies with their petals.
What's there?

---

25. Adam Jerzy Czartoryski (1770–1861). Czart is a Polish word for "devil." Czartoryski was the president of the insurgent government and its minister of foreign affairs. His is associated with Talleyrand because of his belief in the effectiveness of diplomatic rather than military solutions, and he did gain some positive effects by his diplomatic skill.

26. Allusion to General Jan Skrzynecki (1789–1860), one of Chłopicki's subordinates, who took a solely defensive stand (like a crab or a snail) during the Insurrection. The cock crow is a less direct allusion to Peter, who betrays Jesus before the cock cows.

Kordian

DEVILS

An old man, like a lark[27]
Frozen in a block of memoirs,
Half of him preserved, half rotting
Poet—knight—an old man—nothing.
A eunuch for the nine bright stars
In Apollo's harem... [28]

SATAN

Hurry!
Already bells in Cracow's tower
Begin to toll the morning hour
Off to pray the people scurry,
The churches stink as incense roasts.

WITCH

Your work be damned! This gale of hot, vile air
Has shaved my lowly hut of its straw hair;
Will you tile my roof with Communion Hosts?
The willow twigs were stripped by howling storms,
Palm Sunday will have none, after this weather.[29]

SATAN

We're wasting time! Shut up, you worm!
Let's make the rest of them together.
Throw what I say into the kettle.
Take the rust that lies
On Omphale's needle

---

27. Julian Ursyn Niemcewicz, poet and memoirist, companion to Kościuszko, and sympathizer with the conservatives of the November Insurrection. Ignacy Krasicki, one of the greatest of the Enlightenment poets, had called Niemcewicz a lark and addressed a fable to him in that name.

28. The nine muses.

29. Witches are associated with pagan practices that have lingered into the Christian era. One of these is flogging oneself with birch branches during the spring holidays, which coincide with Palm Sunday.

Kordian

From Hercules's bloody fingers;[30]
From this rust there will arise
Foppish knights—malingerers

DEVILS

A crowd, a crowd flies down to earth
Like a cloud...

SATAN

Hurry, bring more men to birth,
Ere morning tears our gloomy shroud;
Before the elements grow cool,
Throw in the tongue of Balaam's ass;[31]
So those who rise up from this pool
Will seize the national dais.
Of orators they'll have no dearth.

DEVILS

A crowd, a crowd, flies down to earth,
Like a flock of storm-swept starlings!

SATAN

Do you see that ashen darling?
Half formed already in the kettle's dregs;
His gaze has withered in the sediment;
Swaying to and fro on his crooked legs,
Just like a shaky form of government.
His mouth is open, hungry for some thoughts,
He only chokes on bookstores and on moths.
He wants to speak. Let's see what seeds he'll sow!

---

30. Omphale was queen of the Lydians, to whom the hero Hercules was bound as a slave for three years as punishment for his madness and the consequent killing of his own wife and children. Hercules fell in love with Omphale and wore women's clothing and did needlework while Omphale wore the lion skin. The reference is to émigré charges of effeminacy against the superior officers of the army.
31. In Numbers, 22:30 Balaam's ass speaks, warning him of the presence of an angel.

Kordian

CREATURE *poking his head out of the cauldron*[32]
Is it good for us to have a king, or no?

SATAN
Away with you, Sphinx, away with your riddles![33]
The very devil cannot find solutions;
Ask those at academic institutions
Immersed in history up to their middles;
From your ministerial seat,
Above the fertile bloodshed of the Nile,
With ruined columns at your feet,
You'll babble in the hieroglyphic style.

ASHTORETH
Lord, look! There in the kettle's steam
Another creature hatches,
He wears a monster's horrid mien,[34]
As well as general's sashes.

SATAN
Behold him! This is our creation!
Destroyer, like the Golden Horde.[35]
The cannon of the capital his station,
A bloody forehead, traitor to his word!
When cannon roar into the dark,
He casts aside the dying knights,

---

32. The historian, Joachim Lelewel (1786–1861), accused in émigré circles of dampening the enthusiasm of the young insurgents and taking an indecisive stance on the dethroning of Nicholas I.
33. The sphinx is a mythical creature with the head of a man or woman and the body of a lion and sometimes the wings of an eagle. The sphinx that plagued Thebes asked each passer-by to solve a riddle: "What walks with four legs at morning, two at noon, and three in the evening?" Oedipus solved the riddle by answering "Man," and the sphinx committed suicide.
34. General Jan Krukowiecki (1769–1850), last commander of the insurgent army. He entered negotiations with the Russian army and then surrendered Warsaw to them.
35. The Tatars (or Mongols) who overran much of Eastern Europe in the thirteenth century.

And like the raven, flees the nation's ark,[36]
And never makes a return flight...
Delivering his country to the sword.

VOICE FROM THE AIR
Begone from here! In the Name of the Lord!

The DEVILS *all disappear*

CHORUS OF ANGELS
The Earth is a stain
On infinite heaven;
A dark star shines among eleven,
Th' eternal grave of Adam's strain.

ARCHANGEL
Upon a time, there was a star that veered
From course in the eternal edifice.
I gave chase and felt its heart beat with fear,
Like a bird caught by trapper's artifice;
I lay down trembling at the Lord's high throne.
God spoke to me in world-creating tones:
"Your wings are stained with human gore."
I fell on my face and embraced His knee,
On the carpet of rays from the starry floor.
"O Lord God, hear me!
I must have brushed my wings against the skin
Of Earth. I saw that blood was spilled about
A tribe lies buried for their fathers' sins,[37]
The people dying... The star going out...
I flew away... and the people expired.

16

---

36. Cf. Genesis 8:6-12
37. The reference is to Poland, and the "fathers' sins" probably refers to the chaos that resulted from the "golden freedom" of the gentry. Though such accusations become common later in the nineteenth century, they were quite rare at this time. Such sentiment conflicts sharply with the image of Poland presented in the same year in Mickiewicz's *Pan Tadeusz*.

Raise them up; Lord, or destroy them with fire.
And if You will not save them by your hand,
Let loose more blood than tears to flood the land[38]
Have mercy on them, Lord!"
"My Will be done!" was God's word...

CHORUS OF ANGELS
The Earth is a stain
On infinite heaven;
God will crush it or blow life within
As with Adam's statue made of clay.[39]

---

38. Calling for an insurrection instead of silent suffering.
39. God creates Adam by fashioning a clay figure and blowing life into it. "Clay," representing man and earth, grows into a major motif of the play.

Prologue

FIRST PERSON OF THE PROLOGUE
O Lord, reach down into the crystal stream
Of consolation. Send a peaceful dream
To your people cut down in battle. Keep
The ghost of despair from troubling their sleep.
Spread a quilt of rainbows for their protection
And wake them not until the resurrection!
To me grant sleepless torture and a fountain
Of tears. Let me stand upon the mountain
And blow the horn on judgment day, alone,
Whoever I will call before your throne
Let him stand before you! God give me pow'r
That when I touch my finger to his brow
It leaves behind the searing mark of Cain,[40]
And in the flames of Hell he shall remain!
I'll fatten up these golden calves, Oh Lord,[41]
And later crush them with a single word.
I will erect a statue made of bronze
And shatter plaster statues with my wand.
Who am I? is the question on your lips:
I'm the spirit of the Apocalypse!
On me your misty eyes should be transfixed
I stand mid seven golden candlesticks,
I have the form of man. My robe flows down
About my feet; a golden belt around
My waist. My woolly hair is white as snow;
And sparks are flashing from my eyes, which glow
Like diamonds. Just like copper from the flame
My legs glow red. My voice roars out its name
Like rushing water seething with the swell,

18

---

40. Viz. Genesis 4:15.
41. When Moses returned from Mount Sinai with the Ten Commandments, he found the Israelites worshipping a golden calf. Moses was angry and smashed the tablets. Exodus 32.

My hand holds seven stars, and when I yell,
A two-edged sword bursts forth between my teeth,
My face is flashing like the fiery wreath
That is the sun's corona. When you fall
Before me on the ground, to you I'll call:
"I am the first... and I will be the last..."[42]

SECOND PERSON OF THE PROLOGUE
For you I'll unravel this poet's vast
Passion, so that you can laugh at his zeal...
Who is he, anyway? What's his appeal?
Is he a twirling dervish, chanting ditties?[43]
Those seven candlesticks are seven cities;
An exile, he has lived in seven nations.[44]
His eyes are flashing from his inspiration,
His raven hair has turned white not from age
But from worry. The stars he has encaged
In his hand are the thoughts where brightness dawns;
The two-edged sword in his mouth corresponds
To a dagger of words, that can, with ease,
Be directed against his enemies,
But silly fools may also feel its sting.

THIRD PERSON OF THE PROLOGUE
At odds with them both, I come from the wings.
Give me the ashes enclosed in the urn
Of the nation. I will arise, in turn,
From the ashes—and then I will set down
My buskins atop the burial mounds.[45]

---

42. This line, like much of the imagery in this speech, is paraphrased from Revelations.
43. Dervishes are members of an Islamic religious order known for their chanting and twirling. The crescent is the Turkish symbol; thus this relates to the crescent moon and its connection to the devil established in the previous section.
44. The First Person of the Prologue represents Mickiewicz or a more universalized poet of his type. Mickiewicz had been an exile for more than a decade when this play was published, but many other poets had also found themselves in that position after the Insurrection.
45. The elevated shoes worn by Greek tragic actors to make them more prominent on the stage.

Kordian

My actors will stand taller than these tombs.
I'll tear off the knights' shrouds within those wombs,
Replace them with the blue of Polish sky.
Their souls will be lit with the dawn of new
Hope, so that the knights will stand before you
With smiles of hello, and tears of goodbye.[46]

---

46. This begins another strong motif of the play, the rising of the Polish dead from
their graves or burial mounds. These lines have been connected to the raising of the
dead presented in Ezekiel 37.

PART 1
ACT ONE

Scene 1

*KORDIAN, a 15-year-old boy, lies under a great linden tree in
a country garden, GRZEGORZ, an old servant, is behind him
cleaning his hunting rifle. On one side a country manor is visible,
on the other a garden, behind the courtyard garden is a pond, a
field, and a pine forest.*

KORDIAN *lost in thought*
A young man killed himself... And panic first
Put words of condemnation in my mouth;
I took it as a kind of gloomy warning
To fast extinguish all my fiery thoughts;
I now despise those silly common cautions,
Despise the admonition. I caught fire, I burn.
With petals raised to heaven, like a flower,
I seize the air and gobble up impressions.
For I can read the thoughts of God in creatures
Of the earth. I can ask the very stones
About the spark that makes the flame.
As this pond reflects the sky it can feel
The very thoughts of heaven.
This quiet autumn, gently swaying trees,
Poisoning their leaves,
Scattering rose petals,
Like the angel of death,
Says softly to the trees, "It's time to die!"
They wither—And they fall.
Thoughts of death from nature
Descend upon my soul:
Melancholy and pale
As I watch the flowers die,
I feel as if the wind is scatt'ring me.
Be quiet, now. I think I hear the sound

Kordian

Of stray sheep bleating in the meadows, there.
The hoarfrost crunches as they trod the grass
And turn their heads towards the whitened sky
As if to ask, "Where have the flowers gone?
Where are the blooming poppies from this land?"
In cold, desolate, silent tones.
The village church bell, with a sound like glass,
Is summoning the folk for evening pray'r;
It calls no prayers from the hardened grass,
The Earth prays only when the sun revives it.
I stand alone here like a tree that's withered
From root to twigs. My lusts and my emotions
Hang on me like so many dried up leaves;
A clump blows off with every gust of wind.
Emotion's goal—to wither;
Emotion's voice is noise;
Devoid of harmony...
Let the multitude call from within me!
Let the crowd of thoughts flare like one great thought...
Lord! Take this petty unrest from my heart,
Give life a soul and then predict its purpose.
Set fire to one great thought and let it blaze,
And I'll become its instrument, a clock,
I'll show it on my face and tick its beat,
I'll chime in words and make my life complete.

After a moment

I'm saturated with unhappy love.

He thinks, then suddenly turns toward GRZEGORZ

Stop cleaning that rifle, Grzegorz...

GRZEGORZ

                              I'm done.
What is it you wish?

KORDIAN

                      Come here, old man...
I'm bored...

Kordian

GRZEGORZ

       Same old story. What should I do?
Would you like to hear a fable, my lord?
A tale lies in this casket of a brain,
My dear departed grandma put it there.
Would you rather have me sing or recite?

   KORDIAN does not answer, and GRZEGORZ recites the
   following fable:

There was a pretty lad in school,
And Janek was his name.
His teachers took him for a fool.
He took to drinking to his shame.
He should have drawn a soldier's pay,
He had no taste for letters.
The master beat him every day,
His birch was torn to tatters.
After at least a hundred blows,
He went to Janek's Ma and said,
"I've beaten Janek on the head,
But nothing sinks in. He must go!"
She took her Janek from this beast,
And went for counsel to a priest.
Before the priest she told her tale,
And sobbing made her body quake;
He frowned and gave his head a shake,
As he attended her travail.
And then he turned upon the lad,
And told him, "Look me in the eyes!"
"He's good for nothing, only bad!"
Gave him a crowbar and a Host,
And told his mother, "I advise
That you find him a cobbler's post."

His words did not fall on deaf ears,
She found a cobbler living near
But it was not to Janek's taste
To strain his eyes on cobbler's thread,
The devil noticed, and with haste

23

Put dreams of wonder in his head.
He gave in to these reveries,
Deciding to use thievery,
And with the crowbar made his way.
The cobbler kicked him out one day,
He swam off to the nearest town,
And everyone assumed he'd drowned.

The mother wept and wrung her hands;
The priest, he would not hear of it,
He thundered from his high pulpit
Against such children and brigands.
He later said, to calm her down:
"He who must hang will never drown."

Well now it's very hard to say
What actions Janek took meanwhile,
He hopped a ship and sailed away,
To a far-off populated isle.
He met the ruler of the land
And bowed before the king's fair dame,
And to the court he did the same,
He knelt down low and kissed the sand.
In greeting, then, the old king rose
And placed his glasses on his nose.
His subjects, following the king,
Then did exactly the same thing.
The king, you see, was far renowned
For his great gift of prophesy;
Although his left side eye was sound,
Yet with his right he could not see.
But still his one eye saw so well
That he could look but once and tell
Whatever fitted you to do,
If you could counsel governments,
Keep ledgers, or else cook a stew.
But then, in spite of his intent
The king's eye failed him in his quest,
He could not see what would be best,
For him to dance or counsel state.

And so he asked him, "What's your name?"
"It's Janek."
           "Janek, what's your trade?
What can you do to bring you fame?"
"I know how to make shoes for dogs."
"And can you say in honesty
You do it well?"
                "Your majesty,
I'm sure that I can guarantee
That I can warmly fit their paws
In winter. And in summertime
I'll make shoes of a single seam
With workmanship of such a kind,
That you can let them cross the swamp,
And never let their feet get damp."
"Well then, you're hired. I'll pay you gold."
The gracious king said to the boy.
So Janek went, as he was told,
Into the palace, full of joy.
And four days afterward at dawn
The hounds went hunting in their shoes.
As for the cobbler, he had on
Silk clothes, same as his retinue;
He wore a gold medallion;
He rode a prancing stallion.
In three days he was Chamberlain,
In six he was a Counselor,
In twelve days he became a lord
And ruled his very own domain.
He sent out for his mother soon;
She's made a lady by the king.
The priest received another boon,
And now he wears a bishop's ring.

KORDIAN
Ha! ha! ha! Yes, that was a splendid story!

GRZEGORZ
Now look, I didn't tell it just for fun,
A lesson's to be learned here in this tale!

25

Kordian

KORDIAN
What lesson? Tell me, Old Man.

GRZEGORZ
                          Just look
For it yourself. I tell you it makes sense!

KORDIAN
And I believe you.

GRZEGORZ
                       Yes, you must believe!
You see, young master, when old servants speak,
Their words are never poison to a child.
I wandered long and far away from home,
I grew so weary with my homesickness
That all the other soldiers laughed at me;
Cutting with my sword gave me little joy
For laughter bears no fruit when it is sown,
But sadness lives forever in the heart,
A learned book that tells its many tales;
A man is not a toadstool, he won't rot
Beneath the pines. But sorrow after sorrow
Collect beneath his nails... I was in Egypt! [47]
Should I talk about that battle?

KORDIAN
                       Please do!

GRZEGORZ *twirling his mustache*
The devil take that mighty man, the corp'ral!
He led the army out into the field...
No not the field, the sand, flat as a board,
On all sides open, as you look around
Your eyes would wander over all the sand
Until they turned to search the sky for God.
He formed the troops into five battle groups
And threw them to the desert like five stars.
I shined in one and saw the other four.

---

47. As a soldier of Napoleon during his 1798 Egyptian campaign.

Kordian

You should have heard us laugh before the battle,
For at the tail end of the army train
Trailed donkeys with the baggage... and with them
Were scholars dragged from France, and they would write
Some pretty fairy tales down in their books.
How we despised this swarm of shrill mosquitoes!
That pack of hounds that sniffed at every stone,
As if they might be rooting out some truffles.
And so we shouted: "Asses and you scholars!
Go hide yourselves within our formations;"
By God, they took advantage of our words.
Although a hardened soldier, I admit
That I was quite depressed before that battle.
The blue Nile flowed afar, as I recall,
We saw the walls of a city beyond;
A cloudless sky stretched out above our heads,
Although the air was clear, it tricked our eyes,
Like candle flames above a catafalque.
But what was most amazing to our troops
Were the magnificent masonry mountains;
It seemed like you could touch the clouds from there,"
Or see the far Carpathians of our home.
Our leader came on horseback... "Vivats" sounded,
Alas there was no wine for all these toasts.
He pointed to those mounds and cried, "Soldats!"
That's French for "Soldiers!" Yes, I heard him say,
"Look over there, you noble warriors,
Down from the summits of those pyramids
A hundred centuries are watching us!"
I looked where he was pointing, and I swear,
Though some, I'm sure, will think me but a fool,
That on the summit of the pyramid
There stood a knight in silver shining armor,
Just like the icons of Archangel Michael, [48]
And he was striking with his fiery spear,
Down at the dragon writhing in the desert,

27

---

48. The archangel Michael is the emblem of the Ukraine, much of which was part
of the Polish Commonwealth before the partitions.

That was descending on us in a cloud
Of dust. A hundred cannon roared and I
Was blinded by the flash. And when my sight
Returned, I saw the Mamelukes descending, [49] ·
Like ravens pecking at us, with curved swords;
With horses turned around as in retreat,
They sat upon our bayonets like monkeys.

KORDIAN
And so? What happened next?

GRZEGORZ
                              Oh, shame on you
For asking. Doesn't everybody know
We always won whenever stakes were high?
And if it wasn't for that cursed plague
But you're not even listening to me…

KORDIAN *pensive, talking to himself*
Yes, shame on me! I am ashamed indeed.
The old man lit a fire within my soul,
This burning thought has often been with me
While walking through the darkest of these woods.
I seem to hear the sound of clanging swords,
Amid the whispers of the swaying pines,
I see myself amid enchanted lamps,
Surrounded by shining battle arrays
That have risen from the bowels of earth,
Like a city emerging from lava…
Such childish dreams!… Such great stupidity…
I'd never dare to show my fantasies
Before the common sense of older men,
So instead I search—for what? A servant
To spin me yarns with long thread.

        He thinks, then suddenly to GRZEGORZ

---

49. The Mamelukes were members of a military caste originally composed of
slaves from Turkey, who held the Egyptian throne from 1250 to 1517. Their power
continued in Ottoman Egypt, and they formed the principal opposition to
Napoleon's forces there.

Kordian

                              Go, Grzegorz!
And if you see a young lady out riding,
Come back and tell me.

GRZEGORZ
                    Did you get enough
Sleep last night, young master, that you could drive
Away this old man as if he was only
Some sort of despicable animal?
I knew a young man when I was in prison
Who didn't despise me, despite his schooling;
He always thanked me for telling my tales,
When I had told them well. He was a noble
And handsome lad, but still his end was sad.

KORDIAN
He's dead?

GRZEGORZ
      What makes you ask?

KORDIAN
                    Then he's alive!

GRZEGORZ
No, he's dead! When the Russians captured us
In 1812 they drove us like a herd
Into Siberia...[50] We were two hundred:
The rotting carcasses of old campaigners
Led by a handful of young officers;
A pleasant memory in my old age
Is how we always called each other "Brother,"
And broke our bread as if it was Communion;
Huddled under the same sheltering cloak.
The name of my young hero was Kazimierz.
Whenever the Muscovites preyed on someone,
Master Kazimierz suffered for us all.
Then an idea came into his head,
To secretly gather us all together

---

50. After Napoleon's disastrous expedition into Russia, in which many Poles served.

Kordian

And tell us his plan. Now don't laugh my lord!
He who earns his white hair rotting in prison
Will never turn his nose at mad despair.
He thought he could knock out the Cossack guards,
Take their weapons, and lead the soldiers back
To Poland... But the Cossacks saw right through
These tricks and led us out into the field;
A Bashkir regiment surrounded us[51]
And kept the Volga river at our backs;
The Tatar colonel read the Czar's decree.
It said that all the Polish prisoners
Should be divided into groups of ten and
Incorporated to the regiment.
Our soldiers held each other's hands and yelled,
"We will not go!" We thought that they would shoot us.
Instead those Tatar devils grabbed their ropes
And threw their lariats around our necks,
As if we were a herd of untamed horses!
I'll bear that feeling with me to my grave!
We held hands as tight as strength would allow.
On my right side—no—my left, near my heart
A soldier stood, bent with wounds and with age;
The Bashkir cutthroat wound round him on horseback,
The old man squeezed my hand until it took
The shape of a sword, then he hung there limp;
I looked into his face, and it had turned
As blue as a corpse, his eyes bulging out,
The rope was embedded into his neck.
The Bashkir lashed his horse, it reared and jumped,
The old man broke free and followed the horse,
Dragged across the sand and over the flint...
I saw a hank of white hair flecked with blood
Sticking on a rock... The horse sped away
Like a bullet... and the corpse disappeared,
But my mind could still see the bloody man
Behind the horse... The rest of us still stood
Like dry sheaves of wheat swaying in the meadow;

---

51. The Bashkirs were a Tatar tribe from the southern Urals.

Kordian

Deep was our silence, our horror, our madness.
The heathens, whistling, drew round us like ravens,
Gouging out our eyes with tugs on their ropes—
Impatient for the hour of death to strike.
Then, Master, Kazimierz, our young Kazimierz,
Leapt out of the crowd at the Tatar Colonel;
He seized him tight and jumped into the river,
He crammed his head between two chunks of ice;
They shifted, and the Bashkir's head came off,
As if he was beheaded by a sword;
It lay there on the ice with open eyes...

KORDIAN
And what about Kazimierz?

GRZEGORZ
                    He was killed...

KORDIAN
And you don't even know his surname, Grzegorz?

GRZEGORZ
No, I don't know. He's famous only under
The name of Kazimierz. What good's a surname
After you're dead? Now will you take the hand
Of your faithful servant?

KORDIAN
                    God! The old man's
Afire with passion, while I have no faith,
Wherever people breathe, I suffocate.
Exploring with a non-believer's eye,
I always return along the same route
From lofty thoughts back to my tortured stream.
I will not walk the path of superstitions.
Now is the time to measure youth with zeal:
"To be or not to be, that is the question..."[52]

---

52. This allusion to one of the most familiar lines in Western literature signals several similarities between Kordian and Hamlet, especially as the Romantics understood him. Not only does it extend the suicide motif, but it also emphasizes Kordian's desire for action and his unwillingness to let love stand in his way.

Kordian

I do not have the strength of Oedipus,
The murderer, to solve the riddles posed
By all the sphinxes over all the world,
And now there are more and more of these sphinxes!
The mysteries of the Trinity[53] are
As grains of sand, or flowers in the field.
The world gets no wider, but does get deeper.
A man can swim, but only on the surface,
The voyage cannot be measured in knots,
And he never knows if his course is true
Once he has gone beyond the sight of shore.
The milestones that he passes on that journey
Are the old superstitions—ashen corpses
Of centuries... Or rather they may be
The crosses placed along the beaten path;[54]
The simpleton tugs at his reins as he passes,
He says farewell, and then he makes a bow...
Later wise men point out a straighter path,
The simpletons slowly change to this road;
Storks weave nests upon the forgotten crosses,
Moss grows and children plant flowers beneath.
And often the crosses, gnawed by long years,
Fall over and kill the children below.
The people will lament their laziness
At forgetting to take the crosses down.
And therefore I now go into the world,
To chop down all of that old, rotten wood.
And what of love?—I will forget its name.
The voice of memories will but remain
Lingering above the storm of the world
Like a crane's song, late in its migration,

---

53. The mystery of the Trinity is traditionally inexplicable by man. Oedipus, who unknowingly killed his father, solved the riddle of the sphinx at Thebes. One way of looking at Oedipus's fate is that he was happy until he had to solve the riddle of his origin. Kordian thus suffers from what we would now call existential angst, which does have its roots in the Romanticism.

54. Crosses or other shrines are erected along country roads, especially at crossroads, where devils traditionally lurk. Passers-by would pause and perhaps say a prayer at these shrines.

Kordian

Gliding across the azure sky alone,
The last of many, distant from his flock.
I need new wings, new paths, new charts.
Like Columbus, I sail uncharted seas,
With melancholy mind and broken heart...

LAURA *calling from the porch*
Kordian!

KORDIAN
       That voice scatters the golden dawn
Of my ambition. I'm trapped in a circle
Of charms from which I will never escape.
I could have been something... I will be nothing...

Scene 2

*A Garden. Linden lanes intersecting on all sides—amid the trees
an abandoned house with broken windows is visible... Autumn; it
is windy, and leaves are falling... KORDIAN and LAURA dismount
from their horses... GRZEGORZ remains with the horses while the
pair walk along the path... They walk in silence for a long time.*

LAURA *with a half-mocking smile*
Why is my Kordian so sad?

    KORDIAN looks at her through gloomy eyes but keeps silent

I found some verses stuck into my album, [55]
I recognized the hand, the pen, the soul.

    KORDIAN blushes and bends down to the ground

Why do you stoop, my lord?

KORDIAN
          To brush away
The thorns, twigs, and weeds from your feet, my lady.
The thorn that pricks my hand, injures no one!

---

55. Laura refers to a poem which she will recite in Scene 3.

Kordian

LAURA
Have you forgotten your dear widowed mother?[56]
What's this? A furrowed brow? A blush, and gloom?

KORDIAN
My lady, it were better that you ask
This tree why its leaves turn purple in autumn
After the hoarfrost has touched it. The secret
Is safe with the frost.

LAURA
                    Let's sit in the lane.
Which one of us will see the first star?

KORDIAN
If it's the star of hope, it won't be me!

LAURA
And what if it's the star of memories?

KORDIAN
Oh, it's much too early for me to see
The delicate, pale star of memory.

LAURA
Well then tell me where is my Kordian's star?

    KORDIAN raises his eyes to LAURA's face then turns away

What's its name?

KORDIAN
              The future.

LAURA *with a smile*
                   What part of heaven?

KORDIAN
Oh, I don't know!—It's a wandering star,
Each day you lose it, each day you must search...

---

56. The fact that Słowacki's mother was also widowed early suggests an autobiographical connection with Kordian.

Kordian

LAURA
You have a shining future: talent, skills...

KORDIAN
Yes, and after I've burned in agony,
The dust of my bones will shine on the masses.
Talent's a lantern in a madman's hand:
Guiding him straight to the river, to drown.
Better turn out the light and close your eyes,
Or buy some common sense and sober thoughts
And forfeit the whole fortune of your dreams.

LAURA
How bitter my Kordian is today!

*She sits down on a sod bench while KORDIAN sits at her feet and
speaks, looking up at the sky*

KORDIAN
Nature is spellbinding! The gray cloud flies,
Like a horse out of the Apocalypse,
Driven by the autumn wind; in the cloud
The very thought of thunder faints with cold,
The sparks within can never escape.
It is the same with me—How can I tell
The world about the anger in my breast?
I'll store my thoughts together with that thunder,
Let them float to the world voiceless and cold.

He plucks a flower and turns to LAURA with a smile

My Lady, take this purple spray of heather,
But do not shake away the frosty diamonds.

Pensive, looking at the sky

Look up at the sky, my Lady, and see
The spirits out of Dante; encircling
The old tree is a flock of startled starlings,
Preparing to alight for the night's rest;
The wind will blow off all the leaves tonight,
But the starlings will sleep right through it all,
Swaying to the song of the dying trees;

Kordian

The angel of foreboding will point out
The path of flight to all the sleeping birds
And when they wake, the tree will tell them, "Fly!
I have no leaves for you, I have grown old
Last night, while you slept."

LAURA

                    And the moral is?

KORDIAN

Ha, ha, but it's sad, the tree didn't sleep
But the birds did...

LAURA

                Kordian, whoever seeks
The future should sleep as well as the birds...

KORDIAN

Well then, where is my angel of foreboding?
Will he come at all, and will he lead us?
Like misers, we must hide away for years
Our feelings and our thoughts, lest we should lose
All our senses in one violent storm.
To see tomorrow we must win today.
Strange curiosity for life leads us
To make this journey. We must pay for it
With our misfortunes. But still we should never
Lose our senses in one violent storm.

    Abruptly

But I've lost mine! Lord, have mercy on me!

LAURA

Kordian!

    KORDIAN does not respond

        It's time for us to head back now,
It's getting dark and windy...

KORDIAN

                Lady, stay...

Kordian

LAURA
Then will you promise me to calm down?

KORDIAN *madly*

                            Yes...

LAURA
The future is a long way off; we're young
And everything is still ahead of us...

KORDIAN
The dark blue sky is shining through the mists,
Look at the moon, my lady, silver, full
And watching us, while silv'ry bits of wool
Torn from the clouds are falling over us;
A rotting branch now cuts the moon in two,
It hides its gloomy face amid black leaves
My lady, there will come a time in autumn
When the white face of the moon shines amid
The sailing clouds; then you will drive away
My wretched, hated shadow from your gaze.

   After a while

The Lord incorporated a mere glimmer
Of the soul within his unfinished work,
That soul was dispersed into colorful
Sensations; and the five senses were taken
From them to serve the body, the rest merely
Extinguished into nothingness... But wait!
Another world exists where these sensations
Are poured together to form a white angel,
Smaller, perhaps, than a man, a mere atom,
The center of a radiating wheel,
A pure, clear light with heart unstained by man.
The soul will then multiply through the sense
Of infinity, and then God will open
The angel's eyes to the future, until
He stops staring at memory's dark coffin.
The Lord will topple a column of light
At his feet while the sun and myriad stars

Will burn all around it. With hopeful gaze
The angel will watch them through to the end.
Then like the stars he'll swim into the future
Oh, how my soul would like to be so toppled,
My wings are now unfurled. My soul will fly
Out of my burning mouth, up to the sky...

Lowers his hands and in despair

We need two earthly souls for one such angel! [57]

LAURA
It's bad for you to be inflamed by dreams,
I don't understand what's wrong?

KORDIAN *scornfully*

I've gone mad...

LAURA goes out to the garden gate, mounts her horse... and rides away with GREGORZ. KORDIAN remains alone and motionless in the garden.

38

KORDIAN
The night lights twinkle in the sapphire sky
My mad thought tumbled into the blue heavens
Where stars have snatched it up into their dance,
They twirl it until, tired and pale and sad,
It returns from the ball to my bored heart...
I wait—standing at the brink of the abyss
Of heaven, frightened at the sight of my thought
Drowning in a swirling starry whirlpool.
You're flying off, stars, like a flock of cranes!
I'll fly with you, into the sapphire sky!

He pulls out a pistol

It's loaded. Good! Then let flint fall on iron...
A moment of pain—then darkness—and then

---

57. This passage follows the mystic philosophy of Emanuel Swedenborg (1688–1772), who suggested that two who are very much in love on earth will unite after death to form a single angel.

Kordian

A blinding light... But what if nothing flashes?
And pain just passes? And everything
Just scatters in one brief moment of pain?
Leaving only darkness... and even darkness
Disappears?... Nothing, nothing—not an I
To tell myself that there is nothing left
No I to even ask God why there's nothing?
Then will I be the victor over nothing?
Death is staring at me with two faces,
Like the sky above reflected in a pond...
Truth or illusion—but who can decide,
When we can't understand? [58]

Puts the weapon to his head

                         No, no... not here
In this garden... I will go to the woods
To find a flow'ry, isolated meadow.

He leaves the garden

Scene 3

Night. LAURA alone in her room at a lamp

LAURA
Eleven has struck and Kordian's not back.
A hideous anguish eats at my heart...
Could I have killed the boy with thoughtless gibes?
Can I still smell the sun-dried, fallen roses?
And if his heart is cast of such a metal,
Will what I write remain eternally?
Oh God! What if his eyes become accustomed
To darkness and to tears? Or worse! What if
Instead of tears that pride, to which such fiery
Youths are prone, stamps bitter smiles upon his face...

---

58. This is a kind of inversion of Hamlet's "To be, or not to be..." soliloquy. Hamlet
fears the afterlife; Kordian fears that there is none.

Kordian

She reflects for a moment, picks up an album, and turns the pages.

These pages filled with boring courtesies.
This one compares me to a flow'r, and these
Compare me to the stars, the fourth makes me
The goddess Diana, while he bears the head
Of an animal, like the god Apis,[59]
And this a flower that would like to bloom...
My sister's picture. Oh! There's Kordian's hand;
I've seen it by chance, but now I must read...

She reads Kordian's verse

"I will sail to an archipelago
Of memories... and stop short of my goal...
Till you say, 'Wretched spirit, Oh
How your quiet soul weighs upon my soul
Like the eyes of the moon on the dark sea,
You're everywhere, above, around, and in me...'
Beloved, I am on, around, and in you...
'I will not come to blame nor reminisce,
I do not dare to curse nor wish to bless;
I've merely dreamed some questions while entombed...
Once you were glad to take a fiancé,
Show me the gold engagement ring!
Has it turned black? It's not my fault, I say!
Why is your hair unbraided and cascading
About your pale face? Something flashes there!
Could it be a strand of pearls
Amid the mist of your hair?
Perhaps a glint of diamond or cobalt?
Or sunny topaz hidden in your curls?
Or is it tears? You're crying? Not my fault!...
Oh Angel mine, you once entwined
Beautiful flowers in your hair,
Before they faded you would find

---

59. Diana is the Roman goddess of the hunt and the moon, the virgin sister of Apollo.
Apis was a bull honored as a god among the Egyptians and associated with the sun.
Bulls are associated with fertility and passion—thus, the essential dichotomy.

Replacements for them everywhere.
But now your hair's no longer braided so?
The flowers have survived the stormy weather
Except for one pale rose, so long ago!
The reason why I can't recall,
Which withered forever
If they all have withered? It's not my fault!"

She stops reading

Hoofbeats... It's Kordian... I'll open the window
No, that would make me seem overly anxious...
Will no one open the door?

Opens the window

Oh my God!
A horse without a rider... What is this?
I'm trembling...

The chambermaid enters

Where's Grzegorz?

MAID

I don't know, Miss.
He never came to supper. You could tell
Because he never touched the jug that he
Always keeps for himself, never sharing,
Like the Jew with Christ's cloak.[60]

LAURA

Go find him, run!

GRZEGORZ *running in*
A tragedy! The master's shot himself!...

End of Act I.

---

60. This line has confused Polish critics. Clearly it is an example of peasant anti-Semitism, but the reference is unclear. It may be a mistaken reference to the cloak of Christ that the Romans threw dice for at the crucifixion so as not to ruin it by tearing it for division. Of course it was not the Jews who did this, but the Romans.

ACT II
The Year 1828
The Wanderer

*St. James Park[61] in London. It is evening. KORDIAN sits under
a tree near a meadow, further on there is a pond shaded by trees
with flocks of birds—near the park are palaces and the two
Westminster towers. [62]*

KORDIAN

A meadow island on the palace steppes... [63]
I fly here to escape the seething crowd;
These folk prefer to drink coal smoke and stare
At shops; while London's enchanted idyll,
This garden, has been lost just like a golden
Digression set within a boring poem.
People! Come and take a look at these trees,
God's miracles near those of your own hand.
These untrimmed trees conceal heavenly graces;
They wind the fog above into black balls
And cool the city with their leafy fans.
The swans sail on the pond with wings unfurled.
Men have strewn these paths with Pactolian sand, [64]

42

---

61. St. James Park is kept in a natural state.
62. Westminster Abbey is where the bodies of England's kings and poets are buried. Below, the Caretaker claims to have a brother who sells these graves, implying that a bribe can buy a poet's status (or a king's).
63. This double metaphor may be opaque to readers unfamiliar with the steppes, which are semi-arid grass-covered plains found in southeastern Europe and in Siberia. A meadow appearing amidst the steppes is like an island in the sea, and so is this naturally beautiful park amidst the (barren) palaces. This is a very Romantic sentiment, but one which can still be appreciated today.
64. The Pactolus was a river in ancient Lydia with golden sand at its bottom. Gold was obtained from the river until the beginning of the Christian era. In legend, it derived its gold from King Midas who washed in the river to remove his "golden touch."

Kordian

These meadows with the down of Flemish velvet.
There the city, a clock with human gears,
But here is peace; the gardens do not bloom
For humans; the flocks are pearls amidst the green...
There was a time when in my childish dreams
I had built every capital on earth,
Now I see them, and they are quite diff'rent;
My first imaginings, still, are not spoiled,
They have remained with me, like travelogues,
To use as models for comparison.
Naked reality, reward my dreams!
So that I might appreciate myself
Just as I now appreciate the world...
Who knows? Perhaps even I will be called
Into the circle of the fortunate...
I would like to wipe Cain's scar from my brow
One glance at my forehead reveals my sin...

Enter the CARETAKER of the garden with chairs for hire

CARETAKER
A penny for a chair, good sir!

KORDIAN gives the man a shilling and does not take any change[65]

You pay like
A lord but don't know how to sit like one!

KORDIAN
Well, tell me how a lord's supposed to sit.

CARETAKER
A magnate sits on three chairs all at once:
One for himself, the second for his feet,
The last for his hat, and that makes three pence.

KORDIAN
Thanks, brother, I'll consider your advice.

---

65. A shilling was worth twelve pence.

Kordian

CARETAKER

These noble customs are profitable,
Some new reform will surely take it from us.

It grows darker

KORDIAN

A lone man, like a shadow, moves about
Among that stand of trees right by the pond.
He gazes at the moon and sighs, a lover,
His heart is surely poisoned with his cares.
His dreams must have been spun with golden thread,
But now it's snapped, and he must flee the world...
I'd like to meet him... Do you know him, brother?

CARETAKER

A bankrupt who's condemned by court of law.

KORDIAN

Then why does he pace here and not in prison?

CARETAKER

The authorities do not enter houses,
Nor do they track down debtors in the night;
So debtors sleep by day and walk at night.
I thought you too had run afoul of law.

KORDIAN

You wretch!...

CARETAKER

        Dear sir, you pay just like a lord.
I recommend my brothers to your service...
The first, like me, sells chairs in parliament,
The next, like me, sells graves in Westminster;
The third one fashions coats of arms for sale,
On each are scales, a yardstick, and two towers
Just like the ones above the debtor's prison. [66]

---

66. The references here are to those who would buy power and a name for themselves, bourgeois who imitate the nobility and often accumulate great debts in the process.

Kordian

The people call the fourth one Tragic Garrick; [67]
He's had the talent of an ape from birth,
He plays the role of Punch out on the street[68]
And uses Punch's mouth to tell the crowd how
He killed his wife and threw his baby out
A window, then how he hanged the hangman;
Until he falls into the devils claws,
And when the devil takes him down below
There isn't a dry eye in the whole crowd...

Exit KORDIAN.

KORDIAN sits on the white chalk cliffs overlooking the sea, reading a passage from Shakespeare's King Lear

KORDIAN
"Come on, sir, here's the place: stand still; how fearful
And dizzy 'tis to cast one's eyes so low!
The crows and choughs[69] that wing the midway air
Show scarce so gross as beetles. Half way down
Hangs one that gathers samphire[70]—dreadful trade!
Methinks he seems no bigger than his head.
The fishermen that walk upon the beach
Appear like mice: and yond tall anchoring bark
Diminished to her cock; her cock a buoy
Almost too small for sight. The murmuring surge,
That on th'unnumber'd idle pebble chafes,
Cannot be heard so high. I'll look no more,
Lest my brain turn, and the deficient sight

45

---

67. The allusion is to David Garrick (1717–1779), famous actor and co-manager of the Drury Lane Theater.
68. Punch is the hook-nosed husband of Judy in the famous puppet shows. It is short for Punchinello. What follows is a synopsis of the traditional "Punch and Judy" puppet show.
69. "The chough is a member of the crow family, a jackdaw, or here perhaps the red-legged Cornish crow." *The New Shakespeare, King Lear*. Edited by George Ian Duthie and John Dover Wilson. Cambridge: Cambridge University Press, 1968. "Glossary" p. 280.
70. "Aromatic plant that grows on sea-side cliffs; pickled in vinegar, used as a relish; gathered by men lowered and suspended by a rope." *Ibid*. p. 294.

Topple down headlong..." [71]

He stops reading

                Shakespeare, Oh, Great Spirit,
You've built mountains greater than those of God
In setting the abyss before the blind
You bring earth closer to infinity.
I would prefer to have my eyes be blinded
By a cloud, and see the world through your eyes.

He stands

It's vain for genius minds to gild the world,
Reality is waiting at each step.
In fact I am just like that man "who gathers
Samphire" on the cliffs of life, "Dreadful trade!"

Exit.

46

*An Italian villa. A room walled entirely in mirrors, carpets,
vases carved from lava full of flowers. Beautiful environs can be
seen through the window. KORDIAN and VIOLETTA, a beautiful,
young Italian girl.*

KORDIAN
Just let me touch your shining hair, my soul!
Entwine me in your arms and I will bloom
With rapture. Flashing eyes so bright and black
With whites like snowy pearls. So when you cast
A languishing glance, I wilt, fall and faint;
Just so the golden butterfly will die
After feasting on the oversweet rose;
But one glance from your sparkling eyes drives me mad!
So I'll come to life for the length of a kiss.

VIOLETTA
Let go of me, I'm fainting!

---

71. Fragment from *King Lear*, Act IV Scene 6. Edgar's speech to the blind Gloucester. *Ibid.* pp. 91-2.

Kordian

KORDIAN
                   My beloved!
When you fall down into a faint, and then
Repel me with the heaving of your chest
And from your verdant coral mouth there flashes
The fire of an unspeakable expression
In which love joins these voices all together:
The breaking of a string, the sound of shame,
The keening of regret, a groan, a sigh,
And children's laughter only then, my dear
Will you love me...

VIOLETTA
                More than life! I've abandoned
My lord and God for you. How can you doubt
It, madman?

KORDIAN
           I believe it! I am hanging
On your coral mouth like a butterfly
That hangs upon a rose. Your neck is burning.
But why cold pearls upon this fiery breast?
Tear them off—wait, I'll bite the thread!

VIOLETTA
                      No, stop!

KORDIAN
Pearls trickle down your breasts like drops of water;
But do you fear the tickling of the pearls?
You tremble like a leaf? Do you love me?

VIOLETTA
I've said a hundred times that you are dearer
To me than life; I cling to your clothing
Like dew to a rose. Will you shake me off?
Then I will burst and scatter on the wind.

KORDIAN *growing ever colder and deeper in thought*
Look at that lava vase where flowers grow;
That lava bubbled once, heated by fire.

Kordian

But when it cooled the carver gave it shape...
The world is such a carver, and the heart
Of woman is just so much cooling lava.

VIOLETTA
This stab at our fair sex is undeserving
Of the poor heart of faithful Violetta...

KORDIAN
Beloved! Somewhere in the north there stands
An ancient castle; coats-of arms of all
My ancestors are set above the gate,
The portraits of my forefathers did once
Gaze down upon me from their gilded frames;
The harsh stares of my fathers today
Reach even here, to this Italian villa,
They track and hound me, for I've melted down
The castle of my fathers for its gold,
So you could wear a fillet at your temple.

VIOLETTA
You poison your heart, Love, with ill-timed worries.

KORDIAN
My dear if I could win back palaces
With but a single tear of yours, I would
Not let it fall. Beloved, it suits you
To flash with diamonds, like the Milky Way.
I want to live for centuries with you
Here in this beautiful villa amid
The laurels, waterfalls, and pretty roses,
The mirrors and bronze. But who knows, my dear,
Tomorrow you may open up your eyes
And stare into the face of poverty,
The grimmest phantom... Damn! I must tell you
That everything is lost!

VIOLETTA
                    Oh, Mio Caro,
What does this mean?

Kordian

KORDIAN

                            Creditors at the door!
But love makes riches evanescent phantoms,
I gave you diamonds, now I'll share my heart.

VIOLETTA

My diamonds, yes... Where did I put my keys?

KORDIAN

Be still, my soul, and listen to my tale.
Last night, to stop the seizing of my fortune,
I took your diamonds to the gaming tables;
The game ate all, except my angel's heart!...

VIOLETTA

Angry and in tears
I'm ruined now! He took my jewels away!

KORDIAN   <u>49</u>

You kill me, lover, with your ill-timed tears.
I place your heart above all gifts of gold.

VIOLETTA

You lost my heart together with my jewels!!
Poverty awaits me!

KORDIAN

                        My horse awaits me.

VIOLETTA

Then ride to hell!

KORDIAN

                      My journey's not that far,
My horse has horseshoes worth a thousand ducats;
I won him yesterday on the last card,
I'll rear him up before my creditors
And gallop o'er the fields throughout the night,
With golden hooves I'll pound the silver dew.
At the next town the horse will be unshod,
And with four shoes I'll order up four feasts,
And then I'll do what all young heroes do:
I'll put a bullet in my brain... My lady,

I'll be so bold to ask you to this feast,
And if you would wear mourning for your lover,
I guarantee that it will suit your face...
My lady, will you ride?

VIOLETTA *after a moment's hesitation*
I will, beloved!

They ride off.

A public road. KORDIAN *with* VIOLETTA *behind him ride at a gallop. The horse slips and falls.* KORDIAN *takes* VIOLETTA *down from the horse*

VIOLETTA
                    What happened?

KORDIAN
Nothing much... The horse just threw
Its shoes and fell.

VIOLETTA
                    The horse threw off its shoes?

KORDIAN
It's nothing... I just nailed them on too loosely,
Not nailed exactly, tied with rusty wire,
He lost them on the road...

VIOLETTA *in anger*
                    You snake of Adam!

KORDIAN
My Eve!! Others will take your Adam's place.
I'm glad with all my heart, that when my servants
Are exiled from your villa, with heads low,
They'll travel in my tracks along this path,
And they will gather gold where teardrops fall.

VIOLETTA
I hope they steal the bullets from your pistol!
I hope you die of hunger and of thirst!

She runs back along the road. KORDIAN *mounts his horse and looks after her with a smile of contempt*

KORDIAN
It's true that woman loves me to distraction,
She searches the path for her lover's traces...
Go where you will, my horse, I give free rein..

He rides off.

A hall in the Vatican with walls covered in damask. The POPE *sits on a chair in golden slippers, near him on a golden tripod is his tiara, and on the tiara sits a red-throated parrot. The* SWISS GUARD *closes the door behind the entering* KORDIAN *and announces loudly:*

SWISS GUARD
A Pole, Graf Kordian!

POPE
53

          Hail! Race of Sobieski. [72]

He extends his foot, KORDIAN *kneels and kisses it*

Is Poland always so especially blest?
I offer prayers of thanksgiving for
Your lucky country, for the Czar, that angel,
Extends an olive branch to us, he wishes
Sincerely to preserve the Catholic faith,
For such a gesture we should sing Hosannas!

PARROT *in a thin, raspy voice*
Miserere!!! God have mercy on us!

KORDIAN
I bring a reliquary, Holy Father,
A spot of earth on which ten thousand women, [73]
Old men and children have been cut to pieces,
Nor were these sacrificial lambs provided

---

72. Jan Sobieski, in 1683 as king of Poland, lifted the Turkish siege of Vienna and effectively ended the Turkish threat to Europe.
73. A reference to the slaughter at Praga (a Warsaw suburb) at the end of the Kościuszko Insurrection in 1794.

With Eucharistic bread before their death.
Keep it with the gifts of His Majesty,
Just give me one tear!

PARROT

Lacrima Christi...[74]

POPE *smiling at the parrot and waving his stole*
Begone, you Lutheran! Begone, I say!
Oh, come now, *Filius Poloniae*,
Have you had the chance to visit St. Peter's,
The Coliseum and the Pantheon?
Come to the Basilica this Sunday
To hear a singer in from Africa—
The Dey of Fez just sent the man to me,
Tomorrow from my seat of majesty
I'll make a great sign of the cross for Rome
And for the world, and then you too may see
Whole nations lying in the form of crosses;
The Poles should pray, believe, and trust the Czar...

KORDIAN
Will no one bless this bloody earth for me?
What say you?

PARROT

De profundis clamavi![75]

POPE *tries to hide his confusion behind a smile while shooing
the PARROT*
Go! Get behind me Satan! Off with you!
He'll hop from the tiara to the crosier,
The devil take that bird... Let me tell you
The soul of Luther's doing penance in him;
He's full of adverbs: "Yet," "Because," "Ergo."
Behind a curtain, once, he argued with

54

---

74. Literally "Tears of Christ," also a type of Italian wine.
75. "Out of the depths we cry..." the beginning of the 129th Psalm (130th
by Protestant reckoning) used in the Roman Catholic Church as part of the
Requiem Mass. The Psalm refers to the Babylonian captivity, and is thus doubly
significant here.

Kordian

A cardinal, the Datary's director. [76]
He thought a shrewd and learned doctor answered
His questions! Then the parrot shook her feathers;
The cardinal tore his hair and gave a shriek;
Then she repudiated all his answers
And finished him off in Hebrew, shouting
"Pappe Satan! pappe Satan! aleppe"...[77]
That stupid creature! God sometimes allows
The weak to overthrow the reason of
Goliaths... Go with God, my son, and let
Your nation lose these Jacobin desires, [78]
Take up the psalms and plow your simple furrows!...

KORDIAN *throwing the handful of earth into the air*
I throw these martyr ashes to the winds
With mouth defiled I return to my homeland...

POPE
I'll be the first to curse the conquered Poles. [79]
Let faith bloom like an olive tree and let
The people live in its shade.

PARROT
                    Alleluia!

Exit KORDIAN.

*KORDIAN stands with his arms folded across his chest on the
highest peak of Mont Blanc*

KORDIAN
This is the summit... but I am afraid
To gaze into the dark abyss of the world.

---

76. The Datary is a division of the Roman Curia that deals with indulgences and dispensations.
77. Cryptic (and still unexplained) words from the seventh canto of Dante's Inferno. The words are spoken by the demonic figure of Plutus, Roman god of wealth, who presides over the circle of avarice.
78. The Jacobins were the radical party of the French Revolution.
79. This is an allusion to the encyclical of Gregory XVI after the defeat of the insurrection. However, according to the date at the beginning of this act, this should be Gregory's predecessor, Leo XII.

Kordian

I'll look... No!... Sky above and sky below!
I've become enclosed in a crystal ball;
And if this spike of ice could float with me
High into the sky... I would not feel adrift.
Here I'll unfurl the black wings of my thoughts
Over all the world... But listen! Be quiet!
The prayers of mankind rub against the ice,
Thoughts drift to God along this icy road.
The sound of unclean human voices dies,
But still the sound of all their thoughts lives on.
I'll be the first to die if heaven falls.
What if a puff could burst this crystal sphere
And scatter it in circles throughout heaven,
Even the stars at the elusive border
Would disappear as if they never were...
I'll try it—I will perish with a sigh...

Looks below

Ha! I remember you, you tomb of nations!
The clouds are parting
And icy peaks emerge from them;
There lies a huge forest of pine and oak
Like a clump of moss in the mountain fissure,
And that pale, white spot is the sea.
I will strain my sight—tear open my eyes,
I would like to see a man.
A flock of eagles circles round one peak
A funeral wreath above pearly ice;
A blue river of fissures flows from me
Each to a separate abyss,
They disappear as if into the sea.

I'm a statue of a man
On the statue of the world.

If only I could scale mountains of thoughts
The way I have scaled this mountain of ice,
If I could stand atop the pyramid
Of thoughts and knock my head against the clouds
Of misconceptions to become myself

Kordian

The incarnation of the highest thought...
To think such thoughts and not desire it still?
A disgrace that each man dreads!
To think such thoughts and not be able to?
I'd tear my breast to shreds!
To not be able to? Now that is hell!
I'll fill my heart with the strength of emotion
So that it will overflow to the masses
And fill their hearts over the brink...
Can it flood the throne and sweep it away?
Have I the pow'r to start an avalanche?
When the avalanche threatens villages,
Can it then be stopped by forehead or hand?
Can I, like God on the day of creation,
With but a wave of His enormous hand,
Throw stars above the buildings of the world,
So that they stay in their predestined paths
And never meet the fragile clay of earth
In their celestial navigations?
I can and so I will!
I must call to the peoples, wake them up!

After a pause, with a hesitant expression

Perhaps it would be better to just throw
Myself to the icy abyss below?...

After a pause, at first calmly, then with growing emotion

Enthusiasm fades on worldly roads...
I bought the bitter kisses of a woman...
I lost my childish faith at the Pope's feet...
I had nothing—nothing and still nothing,
Until I bathed in the air and revived
And now I feel alive!
I still can't make this mighty thought shine forth,
I have a statue's beauty, but no torch.
So I must gather fire from all the stars
And braid it into a crown for my brow,
I'll drench my body with the heavenly sphere
So that it sparkles like marble, like ice.

Kordian

My beauty will be like a fairy spirit
I'll enter the cold world, and I can swear
A thousand stars are shining on my brow
Another thousand flashing in my eyes,
That the statue's charm enlarges the nations'
Emotions and provides the inspiration,
Striking hearts like an idea,
Like a miracle straight from God...[80]

But no, a real idea still is needed
Whether it come from earth or from the sky.
As I was gazing down from these stone heights
The spirit of a knight rose from the ice...
For Winkelried[81] has captured all the spears
Of the enemy, offering his breast.
People! Winkelried is resurrected!
Poland is the Winkelried of nations!
Offer yourselves up as a sacrifice!
Though you fall, as of old.
Carry me, clouds! Carry me, wind, and birds!

A cloud carries him off the icy summit

CLOUD
Sit in the mist... Behold Poland, now act!

KORDIAN *flying toward his native land, with outstretched arms, he cries:*
Children of Poland, hear my words!!!

End of Act II.

---

80. This passage is parallel to that of the First Person of the Prologue, but Kordian contradicts it below.
81. Arnold Winkelried was a hero of the Swiss war of liberation from Austria. At the Battle of Stempach (1386) he offered himself as a target for the enemy spears, and created a breach in the Austrian line, allowing the Swiss to rush through. Słowacki wrote *Kordian* while in Switzerland.

ACT III
THE CORONATION CONSPIRACY

Scene 1

The square in front of the Royal Palace in Warsaw. The windows of the surrounding houses are hung with tapestries and full of spectators. A great scaffolding, covered in red cloth, fills most of the square, on it in rows sit well-dressed women... The Zygmunt Column[82] is in the foreground; spectators are sitting on its base. People of various classes are standing around, watching the palace and conversing.

FIRST PERSON OF THE CROWD
Look, my friend, at what stands before the palace...
These scaffolds were erected overnight
By order of our most merciful Czar...
Now if the nation rebels, heads will roll...

SECOND PERSON
What silly fairy-tales you do make up...
This scaffolding is for our lords and ladies
To see the coronation from on high...

FIRST YOUNG MAN
The broad *estrade* is blossoming with ladies.

SECOND YOUNG MAN
"*Estrade!*" How pretentious! I'd much prefer
Our own word, "platform!"

---

82. A tall column near the Royal Palace, topped by a statue of Zygmunt III. A famous Warsaw landmark.

Kordian

FIRST YOUNG MAN
> I agree, my purist.
But look: feathers, flowers, parasols, tulle
A veritable meadow... Were I but
A worm that I might crawl among those flowers.

SECOND YOUNG MAN
You'd rather be the Czar and walk upon
Their heads.

COBBLER
> Ugh! It's so stuffy in this crowd!
That fat brewer left a big space behind
When he staggered to the Zygmunt Column.

NOBLE
I think that he's the one the Grand Duke ordered
To pull a barrow like a horse for some
Offense; he got so hungry and so skinny
That he could even see his knees, and then
He broke down and cried.

COBBLER
> Why did that man come?
These drums and trumpets play out his disgrace.
He must have filled his belly with gunpowder
To explode at the foot of the Czar like a bomb.

NOBLE
The cobbler understands the rule of honor
And how a man must gain revenge at last.
At last... My pun fell flat—Oh stupid people!
He did not understand my pun! You wretches!
Who buys your scepter buys a shepherd's crook...

COBBLER
Ha, ha! The nobleman is turning red!...

FIRST PERSON
Be quiet! Listen! They're shouting in front!
The Emperor is coming! Let's shout too!

Kordian

SEVERAL PEOPLE
Long live the Emperor! Long live the Czar!

FIRST PERSON
I can't see anything... A banner's flapping
In the wind and slowly coming forward.

SECOND PERSON
An old man is approaching, hair all white,
Like thick March frost; he's carrying a pillow
Of gold with a sword resting upon it...[83]

SOLDIER
The Czar's lucky that Polish swords are sleeping
On pillows...

FIRST PERSON
                    Now the Grand Duke runs ahead
To order the choir to begin their song.

A song to the tune of "God Save the King" is heard

SOLDIER
Ha! Ha! Ha! Their throats are puffed out like bagpipes.

FIRST PERSON
Green swarms of chamberlains all trimmed in yellow
Are milling about like bees from a hive...
He's coming!

SEVERAL PEOPLE
            Who?

FIRST PERSON
            The king!

SOLDIER *sings*

                    "God save the King!"

---

83. General Maurycy Hauke carrying the coronation sword. Hauke remained faithful
to the Czar during the insurrection and died at the hands of the insurgents.

COBBLER

Your singing has no rhythm and no sense...

SOLDIER

That's not my fault! A bullet made me deaf
At the battle of Maciejowice,[84]
I realized I couldn't make a marriage
With the queen of trump, and although I had
My forty points, I still went in the hole... [85]

COBBLER

Keep your voice down! What's the matter with you?
With all your talk of kings and queens d'you think
Informers don't know how to cobble shoes?
You talk as if you'd like to start some trouble,
But just remember, when you have no twine
An awl won't fix the hole that's in your shoe...

SEVERAL PEOPLE

Ha! Ha! Ha!

FIRST PERSON

    A bit of leather shut him up!

ELEGANT HUNCHBACK

Gentlemen! Please allow a man to see...

SEVERAL PEOPLE

Hunchback! Hunchback! Make way for the hunchback...
Lift him on your shoulders...

---

84. Maciejowice was the site of Kościuszko's defeat on October 10, 1794.
85. In the card game Bezique (as later in Pinochle) a royal marriage (the king and queen of trump) is worth forty points. The allusion is to Catherine the Great, who had placed her former lover, Stanisław August Poniatowski, on the throne of Poland. Even with this arrangement, Russia still invaded Poland twice in the final few years of Catherine's reign, in 1792 and 1794, the latter ending in the final partition of Poland and its disappearance from the map of Europe.

Kordian

COBBLER
He would let you!
Why everyone already knows the story
Of how one night when he was coming home
He could not jump the gutter, and he did
Not want to get his satin gown all wet.
He waited till an organ grinder came
And asked the crowd to carry him across.
They tied the hunchback to the organ box
As if he were a bundle of dry straw,
But then they took him into all the taverns,
They turned the crank and teased the hunchback so
That he had no choice but to sing along...

SEVERAL PEOPLE
Ha! Ha!

SOLDIER
Laugh at an old man if you must,
But don't you dare ridicule his misfortune.
Where did he go?

FIRST PERSON
The tower over there.

SECOND PERSON
The Czar came by, and we, like idiots,
Watched the hunchback and didn't see the Czar.

FIRST PERSON
Too bad! I guess we'd better move along,
And find the wine they say will flow like water.

The people disperse

Kordian

Scene 2

Inside the cathedral. A huge altar, ablaze with candles. The Primate is saying Mass with a richly adorned retinue. Music plays... The CZAR is standing under a scarlet canopy. On the steps of his throne are Polish state dignitaries and Muscovite generals... The Primate makes the sign of the cross over the people and goes up to the CZAR, giving him the crown. The CZAR places it on his own head—the chancellor gives him the sword of state on a cushion, the CZAR makes a sign of the cross to the four corners of the earth. The Primate gives him the book of the constitution.[86]

CZAR *placing his hand on the book*
I swear!...

A profound silence, once again... The Primate leaves the altar intoning the psalm Te Deum[87]

Scene 3

The Palace Square and the same people as in the first scene. The tune, "God Save the King" is playing.

FIRST PERSON
The Czar's been crowned, he's coming out of church,
He swore to honor the constitution
As if it was a pray'r from the Lord God.

SECOND PERSON
Where's he going? To the palace for dinner?
A king must eat like any animal.

---

86. The Polish Constitution was considered the most liberal in Europe, but it was routinely breached by Nicholas's predecessor, Alexander, after 1819. Nicholas is about to swear to uphold the constitution as part of the coronation ceremony. This scene is justly famous for its symbolic significance and its irony.
87. The ancient Latin hymn of praise and thanksgiving.

Kordian

NOBLE
Do you know what they'll eat?

SECOND PERSON
Your Excellency,
I'm sure he doesn't have to gnaw on bones!
They'll serve him a meal that's fit for a king.

NOBLE
Pheasants for dinner, our laws for dessert. [88]

COBBLER
Go send your riddle to *The Courier*. [89]
Your Excellency. But what was that shout?

FIRST PERSON
Probably the gendarme parting the crowd.

SOMEONE STANDING ON THE COLUMN
Oh no! The Grand Duke's fighting some old ladies.

A DISTANT WOMAN'S VOICE
My baby! Oh, my baby! My dear child!

FIRST PERSON *to the one* STANDING ON THE COLUMN
What was that cry? Your forehead just turned white!

STANDING ON THE COLUMN
The Duke's hit a woman with a baby,
She tripped and the child fell into the gutter;
The crowd is running away from the Duke,
She is standing alone above the child,
Shielding it with her body... What rare courage!

DISTANT VOICE
The baby's dead?

CLOSER VOICE
The baby's dead?

---

88. I.e. he will destroy the constitution he has just sworn to uphold.
89. *Kurier Warszawski*, a Warsaw newspaper 1821–1939.

Kordian

STANDING ON THE COLUMN *to the others*
It's dead...

PEOPLE
And the mother?

STANDING ON THE COLUMN
Who knows if she's the mother?

PEOPLE
Oh! She's the mother! If she weren't the mother
She would run away! What happened to her?

STANDING ON THE COLUMN
Hold on! Two gendarmes are taking her away,
Now they're washing the blood off the sidewalk
For the Czar...

> *The people disperse, despondent... The coronation retinue returns*
> *to the palace. The crowd has thinned and has grown silent—*
> *music plays—it grows darker. The crowd turns its attention to the*
> *cloth that covers the estrade.*

PEOPLE
The cloth is for us! Let's tear it in pieces...

> *It grows even darker. The people tear the cloth apart and walk*
> *around with pieces of the red cloth draped about themselves. There*
> *are still small groups of people drinking around the wine barrels.*
> *A man in a black cloak wanders among them and sings:*

Song of the STRANGER:
Drink the wine, oh! Drink the wine!
Even though you don't believe
That it is a thing divine
Such a bounty to receive
Streams of wine the pavement yields
No one works the vineyard fields
Drink my comrades! Drink you beasts!

Kordian

Though it was before his time
At the Cana wedding feast
Christ turned water into wine,[90]
Nipped the host's shame in the bud,
For His mother's sweet affection

Louder

At His glorious Resurrection
He then changed the wine to blood...
New faith dawns when you wake up,
Drink your wine and go to bed!
We will gather up the cups,
Cast a dagger in its stead.
Then a strong hand will be best
That the dagger pierce the breast...
Drink your wine! Go off to snore!
As for us, tomorrow morning,
We'll be wine to blood transforming
Drinking consecrated gore!

The song ends—the STRANGER exits

FIRST PERSON
Who sang?

SECOND PERSON
    The song echoes all around me...

THIRD PERSON
Let's go home... There's something strange... It's so dark...

67

---

90. At a wedding in Cana, Christ turned water into wine at the request of His mother. John 2.

Kordian

Scene 4

*An underground cellar in St. John's Church, all around are the
coffins of Polish kings, in the background is a small altar. In front
of the altar is a round table—with one lamp and a chair. The
CHAIRMAN of the conspiracy[91] sits alone at the table—in a black
mask with hair as white as snow... Stairs are visible leading up to
the church corridors, a SENTINEL is partially visible at the top of
the stairs.*

CHAIRMAN *alone*
Dark cavern of coffins, I know you well!
Oft have I hidden my thoughts in these remains,
I woke up the kings and guessed at their hearts,[92]
Their counsel: Nowhere in our history
Have kings been stained scarlet under our sky.
If you could rise up from your coffins, Kings,
The People would cry: "Yes, we know you well.
Our fathers told us you were white like angels!"
Will I bloody the pristine Polish throne?[93]
I've thrust myself into the blackest shadows
Of the abyss of foul conspiracies,
I command the daggers of hot-headed youth,
I have a hundred hands, a hundred daggers,
When I want, I can deal a hundred wounds,
My sight grows dim with age, but keen eyes have
My conscience, and I see the lamp is out...
Far better to have died with Washington.[94]

---

91. Słowacki has patterned this character after Julian Ursyn Niemcewicz, poet,
patriot, memoirist, and companion to Kościuszko. In this play he is identified with a
type of old man that dampens the enthusiasm of the young.
92. An allusion to Niemcewicz's Śpiewów historycznych (Historical Songs).
93. No Polish king has ever been assassinated.
94. Niemcewicz (1758–1841) was taken prisoner with Kościuszko after Kościuszko's
failed insurrection. After their release, he accompanied Kościuszko on his celebrated
return to the United States in 1797. There Niemcewicz was a guest of Washington.
Niemcewicz settled in the United States after Kościuszko was spirited away (to meet
with Napoleon) and even married an American woman. He returned to Poland in
1802, however, without his wife.

Kordian

SENTINEL
The Password?

VOICE
Winkelried.

SENTINEL
Down there!

A masked man in a priest's cassock descends to the cellar

PRIEST
I see
The Chairman has gotten here before us.

CHAIRMAN
Don't be surprised to meet me first among
The graves; for old age led me here.

PRIEST
Tell me, Mister Chairman, how will this all turn out?

CHAIRMAN
I do not know...

PRIEST
A storm can't scatter daggers
Like fallen leaves... I hope that we'll succeed!

CHAIRMAN
Remember that you wear the pure white gown
Of Christ our Savior. You will blemish it.

PRIEST
Your voice is trembling.

CHAIRMAN
It's so cold and dark...

PRIEST
But my blood boils...

CHAIRMAN
Lord, have mercy on me!...

Kordian

Tell me, Father, how old are you?

PRIEST

                  Fifty...

CHAIRMAN

Then I was twenty-nine when you were born. [95]
I fought for freedom...

PRIEST

              So?

CHAIRMAN

              Nothing! Memories!

PRIEST

You woke my conscience and troubled my soul.
So, what are your orders? What should we do?

CHAIRMAN *with enthusiasm*

For God's sake, let us put a stop to them!
Do not let youthful thoughts cross the dark threshold,
Don't let the black face of conspiracy
Be seen in light of day, where God's sun shines
So brightly on the world. I've called the madmen
To me here where cold winds blow from the graves,
If need be I can call upon the ashes
Of kings for my defense. Once, from my breast
There flowed a poet's song. Today, I'd gladly
Rip my fame's pages out of history's book
And burn them in the fire, if from those flames
There could arise a thought to drown the noise
Of youth, a thought to shatter all their daggers.

---

95. Since Niemcewicz was born in 1758 and this event takes place in 1829, the ages of the Chairman and Niemcewicz do not coincide. Given the other obvious allusions to Niemcewicz, this seems like a nod on Słowacki's part. However, it may be an attempt to distance his fictional character from the real Niemcewicz.

Kordian

PRIEST
You've started it all out very badly,
Their swords are shining, sharpened on the tombs.

CHAIRMAN
They've sharpened regicidal swords and daggers
On the graves of our kings? What a disgrace!

SENTINEL
Who goes there?

VOICE
                    Winkelried.

*The SENTINEL motions him downstairs and a masked officer
CADET descends*

CHAIRMAN *to the PRIEST,* sotto voce
                                   Support me, Bishop.

PRIEST
I'm recognized... These death-masks have betrayed us.

CADET
How many worms have dined in these kings' coffins?
I'd like to raise the lids, look at the dust...

SENTINEL
The password!

VOICE
                    Winkelried!

The FIRST PERSON OF THE CROWD, masked, descends the stairs

FIRST PERSON OF THE CROWD
                              The Chairman's head
May be all white with age, but it still knows
Just how to pick a place... The church is open

71

Kordian

For Forty Hours devotion to the Czar,[96]
Spy sentries are standing at the church gate
Writing citations for those who come in
To pray for the Czar. So we cannot lose
In killing two birds with one stone, we can
Still love our country and honor the Czar.

SENTINEL
Who goes there? Halt! Who are you? What's the password?

VOICES
Winkelrieds!

A great many masked men of various stations descend the stairs

FIRST PERSON
        Just what does "Winkelried" mean?

SECOND PERSON
Some magic word, like "abracadabra."

CADET
He was once the leader of the free Swiss,
He grabbed the enemies' spears in both hands
Thrust them into his heart and barred the road.

FIRST PERSON
We need a knight of old like that today!

CHAIRMAN
Silence! This is no place for idle talk,
So pray instead! We have come here to these
Catacombs to pass judgment on the Czar!
Look into your hearts! Look into your hearts!
Lest we commit an act of villainy
For future generations. And may God
Surround us with a wreath of starry truth,
Let the angel of silence be with us...

---

96. On special occasions the Sacred Host is displayed in a church for forty hours,
and the church is kept open during that time so that the Host may be adored
by the faithful. The fact that this is done in honor of the Czar sarcastically implies
a sacrilege.

Kordian

SENTINEL
Halt, who goes there?

VOICE
Winkelried!

The general silence is regularly interrupted by the voice of the
SENTINEL *and the answers of the conspirators. Masked men*
in various garments descend the stairs and sit in silence on the
benches. The voices of the SENTINEL *and the conspirators become*
less frequent until they stop entirely... A deep silence ensues until
the clock on the church tower slowly tolls ten o'clock.

CHAIRMAN
Brothers, in
The name of God, our court is now in session.

A moment of silence

FIRST CONSPIRATOR
In the Name of God, I write the word vengeance
With my dagger...

SECOND CONSPIRATOR
As do I.

ANOTHER
And I.

ANOTHER
And I...

CHAIRMAN
I stand before you with gray head, my people,
And tell you to stand fast! My ancient eyes
Have seen great men, and I can tell you firmly
That you are nothing like them! If you hold
Some faith in God within you hearts, my People,
I urge you in the name of God to halt!
Exchange your knives for consecrated swords,
Someday we'll toll the bells of resurrection,
The sound will shake the thrones of kings so they
Will topple like felled trees.

Kordian

CADET

I look into

The darkness of the past and see the shadow
Of a woman in mourning but who is she? [97]
I look into the future and I see
A thousand stars, but this shade from the past
Is stretching out her hand to them, imploring;
These stars are daggers shining bright... I see
Our former country. Something else as well.
The stewards, in their wisdom, then had grafted
A new country onto the old tree trunk. [98]
Now both are blossoming from the same stalk
Like roses of two colors on one bush,
Like two knights wearing identical armor
Attacking their enemy side by side,
Like two pray'rs drowning in the breast of God,
Inspired by one thought, like two swarms of bees
Which keepers pour into a single hive.
Once upon a time, the great Southern Titans[99]
Rose up against God—kings—and slavery.
God only laughed upon His sapphire throne,
But still the kings were toppled like felled poplars
The Guillotine, enshrouded in rag palls
Untiringly kept waving its steel hand,
And with each wave the crowd was thinned by one.
The kings all looked on, for the guillotine
Was a dramatic tragedy presented
By the people with kings for audience.

74

---

97. Polska (Poland), usually personified as a woman because of the feminine gender
of the Polish noun.
98. Lithuania, which was united officially to Poland in the Union of Lublin of 1569
to form The Commonwealth of Two Nations. The May 3, 1791 Constitution was
to have made them into a single state, which would have been the final stage in the
unification process.
99. A double allusion, directly to the Titans of Greek mythology who rose up against
the Olympian gods, and indirectly to the leaders of the French Revolution.

Revenge! Catherine, the harlot and czar, [100]
Had turned her murdering gaze upon us;
She deemed us worthy of a martyr's wreath,
Inventing a new style of martyrdom...
She grabbed the head sliced off the Bourbon torso,
Pale but bloody, and planted it onto
The torso of her bridegroom, then gave him
To us for a king, a corpse-headed king. [101]
Later she stole his dominion of death,
He never lifted a finger to stop it...
With no mourning crepe on our mother's gown
So it was split into three sep'rate parts. [102]
Today, you can ask the gulls flying from
Siberia how many have been groaning
In the mines? And how many others slaughtered?
How many turned traitor, shaming themselves?
But all of us have been chained to this corpse;
For this land of ours is indeed a corpse.
The brother of the Czar [103] went mad, and so
They threw him into Poland, to let him
Tear her apart with rabid teeth, infect
Her with his scum-flecked gums. Conspirators!
Avengers! When the Czar set down his crown
At the foot of the altar, we should then

75

---

100. Catherine the Great of Russia, called the "Great Whore" by Byron, in reference to her practice of taking young lovers, and in obvious disgust at her tyranny toward Poland and other nations under her control or influence.

101. This refers to Catherine's placing her lover, Stanisław August Poniatowski, on the Polish throne. Although in many ways he was a better (and much more liberal) king than his Saxon predecessors, he ultimately joined the Targowica Confederation that opposed the May 3 Constitution and called for Russian military intervention, leading to the second partition of Poland in 1792.

102. Unlike the robe of Christ for which the soldiers threw dice so as not to tear it, the robe of Poland (i.e. the land itself) was divided among the three partitioning powers: Russia, Austria, and Prussia. An allusion to dividing the cloak or robe is also made in Act I, Scene 3.

103. Grand Duke Constantine, known for his outbursts of temper, elder brother to Nicholas, renounced the Czardom, and was made viceroy of Poland.

Have killed him with the coronation sword,
Entombed him in the church, and fumigated
It as we did against the Turkish plague,
And walled up the doors, exclaiming: "O Lord,
Have mercy upon us for all our sins!..."
Just this and nothing more..The Czar is now
At table while our Satraps[104] bow their heads,
A thousand goblets foam with sparkling wine,
The torches blaze and Gypsy music thunders
Knocking plaster from the walls. While our women
Blossom all around, fresh and fragrant as
The Rose of Sharon[105], leaning their fair heads
On Russian shoulders.

Forcefully

Let us go there to
Announce our verdict, burn it on the wall,
The judgment of Belshazzar at his feast![106]
The potion will drop undrunk from the Czar's hand,
And words written in a blue flash of swords
Will prophesy death surer than a Daniel.
Our country will be free! The light will shine!
Poland's borders will extend to the sea,
She'll live and breathe after the stormy night.
She'll live! Can you grasp this word in your soul?
You know... A heart is beating in this word,
I've taken it apart into its sounds,
I've crushed it to individual letters,
Within each sound I hear a mammoth voice!
Our day of vengeance will be epoch-making!
Our joy will be enkindled on our first day

104. Satraps were the governors of conquered nations in ancient Persia.
105. Sharon was a region of Palestine famous for its roses. The image is given erotic connotations in The Song of Songs 2:1.
106. Belshazzar, Nebuchadnessar's son and king of Babylon, gave a feast at which he used the precious vessels taken from the Israelites. A hand appeared and wrote the words "Mene, Mene, Tekel, Upharsin" on the wall. The prophet Daniel was called in to interpret, and he prophesied Belshazzar's demise and the loss of his kingdom. Belshazzar was slain later that night. Daniel 5.

Of freedom, and our cries of happiness
Will strike against the heavens. We will measure
The darkness of our long imprisonment,
And sit upon the ground and cry like babies,
The awesome weeping of the resurrection.

Murmurs of enthusiasm

CHAIRMAN
This pretty picture is a thought from Hell,
Your youthful enthusiasm is holding
You over the abyss; you would not dare
Examine this thought with the eye of conscience:
Look! The Czar lies slain in a pool of blood,
His family also slain... That's the outcome
Of this dire crime... but God will punish us!

CADET
I say let's take the vengeance of the Romans
On this dwarf Caesar. [107]

CHAIRMAN
                    And what will we do
When some Antony shows the bloody cloak
Of Caesar to Europe and calls for vengeance?
When all of the nations descend on Poland,
What army will you use to stand against them?
How many? Armed with what? With bloody daggers?

PRIEST
What will the speaker on the dais say
When they raise the corpse of the potentate,
Who shakes the thrones of Europe with his scepter,
Up to the catafalque, midst clouds of incense
And glowing candles? "People, oh my People!
Let forth a crystal stream of raging tears,
Beat your foreheads to the ground for this land

---

107. Słowacki here alludes to the assassination of Julius Caesar and below to the subsequent stirring of the crowd by Marc Antony. This is appropriate on another level, since the Czar, as the name implies, claimed succession from the Roman Emperor.

Of Lechites. [108] Sprinkle dust and ashes on
Your heads, for this land of Jael is armed,
To its disgrace, with hobnails..." [109]

CADET

That style suits
This man of God. He has already written
The funeral oration for the Czar.
Some wind has turned this weathervane around,
The sermon has a double edge, which cuts
Against us. But the sermon should say also:
"This nation has thrown off its iron shackles
So beat your foreheads, nations, for the Lechites,
And let kings sprinkle ashes on their heads
And let them wail in the streets."

CONSPIRATORS

Ha! Ha! Ha!

CHAIRMAN

Accursed is he who desecrates the graves
Of kings with laughter...

PRIEST

Damned!

FIRST PERSON

They've called us here
To make fun of us to their hearts' content,
Curse us and drive us crazy...

PRIEST

God will not
Allow murder to be planned in his house,
His thunder will roar and lightning will flash
The murderers will burn in fires of Hell!

---

108. Poles. Lech is the legendary founder of Poland.
109. In Judges 4, Jael, Heber's wife, invites Sisera, the leader of the Canaanites, into
her tent as a refuge and pounds a tent nail into his head as he sleeps. The Priest here
uses it as a symbol of a sin against hospitality, which is considered a sacred duty in
Poland.

Kordian

OLD MAN
How many must be killed to free the country?

VOICE FROM THE CROWD
The Czar...

OLD MAN
      That's one...

VOICE
           His wife.

OLD MAN
                That's two...

VOICE
                    Two brothers...

OLD MAN
That's four... Keep counting brother, we'll lose track...   79

VOICE
The Czar's son...

OLD MAN
      Five...

VOICE
           And that's all.

OLD MAN
                  Kill them then!!!
Their blood be on my head...

CHAIRMAN
           You're an old man!

OLD MAN
I will not talk to you... My brothers listen!
If one is not enough to bear this blood,
I'll sacrifice my sons and daughters too.
I'll bear the blood of the woman and child,
My sons will bear the princes, while my poor
Weak daughters bear the light blood of the Czar.
And when God calls us on the Day of Judgment,

Kordian

I will stand beside any potentate
Who wallows in the tears of all his subjects,
And I will say, "See us covered in blood!
We've taken this blood from your people, Lord,
That the burden of their cross would be lighter
In this valley of tears which we call Earth;
We now surrender ourselves to your will..."

CADET

Give me your blessing, Old Man!

PRIEST

                              He insults
The Lord and Divine Justice...

CADET

                              Silence, Priest!
You cannot see this thought flying to heaven...
There's a great lesson in this sacrifice!
This old man breathed new faith in me alone.
Only Satan himself could deceive you
On hearing these words. God will punish me
Hard if these words I sow do not bear fruit.
Believe in me, my people! I am strong!
My sole weakness is locked within my heart,
There the worm of sadness gnaws upon me,
That even while I talk to you I want
To stop and sit and let the tears flow down;
But this sadness is merely childish grief
For nothing, or perhaps for our lost country...
People! You should believe the man who suffers...
Do not take shelter under some great tree
Which age has stripped of all its decayed leaves...

In despair

If I were a lyre, I'd move you with song!
If I were a history book, I'd read
A page about Poland, fortunate, blooming,
And you would all rise up like open graves,
Spewing forth avengers... Enthusiasm

Kordian

Is ripping me apart, my breast is open,
You ought to see the pureness of my heart...
I come not to mislead you like dark angels,
Nor do I hesitate, thoughts split in two,
I'm whole and one... And when I save the country,
I will not sit upon a throne, or near
A throne, or under a throne. I'll burn up
Like incense in a flash of sacrifice!
My charred corpse will not leave behind a name,
Just an echo... and a great, empty space!
And history will owe my name a debt
Of praise it will repay by but forgetting.
Nothing left behind but the pronoun, HIM,
But this nameless pronoun will turn milk sour
In the royal nurseries; baby kings
Will cry and dream about the unnamed spirit
Who tears off crowns... For you there will be life,
A free country, now you will own the thrones;
I'll do this in a moment of rebirth.
Surrender to my hand! Instead of clinging
To the scepter, let us shepherd the strength
Of our great nation! I will then embellish
The crown of Jehovah with that rare pearl:
Our resurrected people... Give yourselves
Into my hands! Pride will not delay me,
Nor will the dreams of lower animals.
Until I can implant eternal freedom,
I will not let a dream come near my eyelids.
Are you afraid that I will let you down?
Then take them off and nail them to a cross,
Like Regulus, [110] eyelids cut off, I'll watch
My country dying, dreamless for all time.
Then carry the suffering cross before you
As an emblem. I will not let you down...
I swear by the shades of my ancestors!

---

110. Marcus Atilius Regulus (third century B.C.) was a Roman general captured
by the Carthaginians, who was sent on a mission to Rome, then, true to his words,
returned to captivity where he was tortured to death, with his eyelids torn off.

And by the sufferings of Christ! Your faith
Will say, "You are the conscience of the land
Arise and shed the Czar's sin from your souls."
I also swear my swearing is in earnest!
As I desire salvation for my soul!
So give yourselves into my hands...

CHAIRMAN
                            My voice
Is paralyzed, I cannot talk...

He sits and hides his face in his cloak

CADET
                        Old man,
Has my enthusiasm bested you?
Behold the first victory... I will conquer!
Or else I will perish in the attempt!
Hey now, Czar! Did you steal our Polish land?
For that you die! You knew as you were stealing
It that the punishment for this was death.
Hey now, Czar! Did you slice it into pieces?
Then take the parts fresh from the guillotine
And hang them from three thrones as from three gallows,
Where royal thieves look on them in disgust?
Hey Czar, if I could kill you more than once,
I'd summon you before God's judgment twice...

*The crowd begins to make noise, raising their daggers and rising
from the benches*

CHAIRMAN *throws the cloak from his head... stands and makes a
hand-washing gesture, then he says slowly and seriously*
Do your will... I wash my hands of this blood.[111]

CADET *to the* CONSPIRATORS
And you?

Long silence

82

---

111. This, of course, is an allusion to Pontius Pilate's action before the Crucifixion.

SENTINEL

     Halt, who goes there? What's the password?,

CONSPIRATORS

We are betrayed! We'll all be killed!

CADET

            Be quiet...

The sound of a falling body

SENTINEL

He didn't know the password...

FIRST CONSPIRATOR

          And his body

Is falling down the stairway.

CADET

         Stop shaking

Now, Mister Chairman, after all you washed

Your hands of all this blood... Well, didn't you?

Give me the lamp...

He brings the lamp near the corpse

        A dagger in his breast...

Some torn and crumpled paper in his pocket...

It's something from secret police headquarters.

A spy... Bury him there in the dark corner.

Two of the conspirators carry the corpse to the corner along with two lanterns and dig a grave

CHAIRMAN

This meeting's adjourned... there will be no other.

CADET

You'd take advantage of this stroke of fate,

Old man? From such a trivial alarm?

Still, I do not despair. Each man will judge

The Czar to be a felon on his own.

How 'bout a vote to see how each man thinks?

To see if zeal or fear will tip the scales?

83

Kordian

CHAIRMAN
So be it... A fine Old Polish custom.
How will we vote?

PRIEST
                God's servant will advise.
Whoever is for the death of the Czar
Let him throw a bullet onto the table!
Whoever's for acquittal put a penny...
There are some pennies in the poorbox here...

> *He throws a coin on the table, followed by the Chairman.*
> *The other conspirators throw coins or bullets by turns,*
> *each landing with a clink*

FIRST CONSPIRATOR
I'll follow the Leader and lose a penny.

ANOTHER
I'm penniless, but I can spare a bullet.
Long live freedom!

ANOTHER
                I won't give a red cent
For the life of the Czar...

ANOTHER
                  We may be buying
Treason, but let the chairman have his way
With our pennies... our time will come again.

FIRST CONSPIRATOR *to the gravediggers*
You grave-diggers, come over here, you must
Decide whether to throw a bullet or
A penny.

GRAVEDIGGERS
            Yes, we know! You made us bury
A dead man, but our feelings are not dead
To the mercy of God.

Kordian

FIRST CONSPIRATOR
They both gave pennies;
I guess they want to get out of this trade,
They don't want to dig the grave for the Czar.
Let's see which way the wind blows from these bellows,
And hear what tune the organ will be playing...

They all come forward in orderly fashion while the CHAIRMAN counts

CHAIRMAN
Shine the torch over here! Thanks be to God!
But five votes for the crime.

CADET
Then the Czar dies!

CHAIRMAN
Young man! Only five bullets were put down...
One hundred fifty were against the crime...

CADET
My sight and life have grown suddenly dim!
I've wagered my whole future on one card,
And lost... The titans toppled from their stilts—
They're merely dwarfs! My brothers, you should look
Carefully at each of these coffin lids.
Does each of these conceal a man long dead?
Or has this skeleton you see before you
Risen up from one of them?

To the CHAIRMAN

When I look
Into your senile thoughts, old man, I see
That you were born into another age;
Why wear this mask? No one on earth knows you.

CHAIRMAN
I never tried to mask my white hair.

CADET
Always the same old song, the old age anthem;
Just like a schoolmaster you sow these lessons
Into the souls of children, so that they
Too will grow white hair. Remember that they
Once had fiery spirits and beating hearts,
But misfortune struck them down, and their hair
Has turned white in a single sleepless night;
So respect them... Stand before them, Old Child...

To the CONSPIRATORS

I predict long lives for the rest of you,
For you knew how to choose a guiding star;
Follow that silver head into the black
Night of captivity —I've lost all hope;
You were gleaned from the crowd, like finest wheat,
But how small you really are... Go away!
I despise you! And if you did not dare
To dedicate yourselves to this great cause,
Perhaps you would not also shrink from treason?
In sign of contempt to you in your masks
I throw my life at your feet... as a gift...

Rips the mask from his face

CONSPIRATORS
It's Kordian! Kordian! Don't you know us Kordian?
There are no traitors here! Look at our faces!

All unmask... KORDIAN *gazes all around, he lowers his head in thought, then, raising his head, he slowly speaks*

KORDIAN
Now Kordian will be the victor among
The noble-minded. You've revealed your faces,
So he will reveal his thoughts and his heart.
I'm on duty in the Palace tonight!
Do you understand? It's me that's on guard
In the Palace tonight!

He goes to the table and writes a few words on a piece of paper and throws it at the CONSPIRATORS

FIRST CONSPIRATOR *reads*
>"To my dear nation
I bequeath all I have: my blood and life,
And an empty throne to be shared by all."

KORDIAN *leans on the altar and looks madly at the silent* CONSPIRATORS, *then waves his hand and says:*
Begone from here, Conspirators!

All disperse in silence... KORDIAN *remains leaning on the altar, steeped in thought... The two gravediggers go out, leaving behind a burning lantern on the mound. The* CHAIRMAN *alone remains—and kneels at the altar behind the standing* KORDIAN.

CHAIRMAN
>Kordian!

KORDIAN *turns and speaks with increasing madness*
Who awakens me? Is the hour at hand?
I remember now... the lantern... the grave...
You dug the grave and now you want your pay?
Take these two ducats which have been engraved with
The Virgin Mary. My mother gave them
To bless her son. You must have children too?
Have your family pray to God for me.

CHAIRMAN
Alas! I have no children!

KORDIAN
>Have no children?
Your hair is as white as new fallen snow;
Then you have not paid God back for your life.

CHAIRMAN
Kordian! I kneel at the steps of the altar,
But not before God, I kneel before you.

Kordian

I've lost the battle with death, but I fight
Another battle with myself, my conscience,
My conscience made me stop the trial...

KORDIAN

Old man!

You pile crime upon crime because you kneel
Before a criminal. Now come with me
I've looked into the book and I will show
It to the world. For Poland's not unworthy
Of any sacrifice... Even a crime...

CHAIRMAN

Oh Kordian, for the love of God, you're ill
With fever, and there's madness in your eyes...

KORDIAN

It's nothing, but my hair turns gray and hurts,
I feel the death of every single hair...
It's nothing... Plant two twigs of poplar and
A rose upon my grave... And then a dew
Of heavy tears will fall and bring my dead
Hair back to life. Now, do you have a pen?
I'd like to write the names of those who'll cry
For me... My father—dead. My mother—dead.
All my relatives also dead. The girl—
As good as dead... No one left behind me!
Everyone is with me! So let the gallows
Be my tombstone...

CHAIRMAN

Look, Kordian, here's the note
You gave to the conspirators. Take it,
And free yourself of all your promises.

KORDIAN

One, two... Right shoulder... Arms! Palace guard duty...
Be alert... Silly words, what are the orders?
Old man, you bore me with your inert face;
I can't forget that I will not grow old.

Kordian

If ever you see me surrounded by
A circle of my children, you must spit
On my gray head.

The clock on the tower strikes eleven

I hear my call from heaven.

He runs out. The CHAIRMAN stretches out his hands after him

CHAIRMAN
Kordian! Wait! I beseech you in God's name!

He exits after him

Scene 5

*The Concert Hall in the Royal Palace, lit by lamps. All around
are marble columns. The walls are painted in arabesques.
Through the open door we can see a long line of dark rooms,
at the end of which a light shines faintly in the CZAR's bedroom.
KORDIAN leans on the bayonet of his rifle. Various phantoms
are present.*

KORDIAN *coming forward with his rifle*
Get away from me! I'm the murderer
Of Czars! Begone! It's time for me to kill.

IMAGINATION
I speak through the eyes, I'll conquer your will.

TERROR
I speak with a heartbeat, your soul to stir.

KORDIAN
What are these voices? No one's there!

IMAGINATION
Don't look at me, but fix your stare.
Where I point!

89

Kordian

KORDIAN
                    I see no trace
Of finger, but my eyes do fall
Upon the image of a face,
Mid the arabesques on the wall.

TERROR
Convince yourself, look close, be bold,
The reptiles move—abominations...
Each of the snakes, in fiery gold,
Coils in a ring-like designation.
The columns shake their snaky manes;
Horrid sphinxes have come out
From the marble, where they strain
To inch forward, crawl about;
Snakes whistle like the wind, the sphinxes wail
Like babies. Don't step on their coiling tails!

IMAGINATION
Like a butterfly, timid, airy,
A maiden has flown from the wall,
A princess bewitched by some fairy,
Or is it nothing at all?
Is she an enchanted princess?
Or herself a vile sorceress? [112]
Remember! You once saw her face!
Remember! She looks so familiar!
But she was gloomy and her gaze
More modest. And this one has stars
Embroidered onto her gown,
Real stars on her sapphire dress,
Little worlds that are shining down...

---

112. On the ceiling of the Concert Hall of the Royal Palace was a painting
by Bacciarelli entitled, "The Unraveling of Chaos." A section of this painting
presents Flora scattering flowers. Here she seems to have come to life (in Kordian's
imagination?) as the legendary Lamia, who, in Keats's version, is a serpent who
takes the form of a beautiful woman. Her exact significance here is subject to some
scholarly debate.

She is the gentle shepherdess
Of the celestial village,
A flower basket on her head,
And as for her bright visage,
An angel's face is in its stead.

TERROR
Look at her eyes! Her steadfast stare!
Where'er you are, she looks at you.

IMAGINATION
Smell the fragrance of her hair!

TERROR
You've stepped upon a snake. It's split in two!
It bursts to pieces!

KORDIAN
                Sweet Mary and Jesus!!!

He rubs his eyes

The dream has vanished... So, forward, forward
With bayonet-fixed to run through the Czar!

He enters the adjoining hallway, which is totally dark. On the left is an open door to the conference room. This room, in the shape of a gilded egg, is lit by moonlight. In the center stands an artistically crafted golden tripod. On it lies the Czar's crown. [113]

BOTH FORCES
Halt!

KORDIAN
        Let me go! God's wrath depends on me!

---

113. This is the crown of the Czar of Russia, which he has also used in his coronation as King of Poland as a conscious act to indicate the unity of these two realms. The later presentation of the blood dripping from the crown is in sharp contrast to the unblemished Polish crown. Several Czars were assassinated and others suspected of being assassinated (as were several Roman Emperors, the Czar's claimed predecessors).

Kordian

BOTH FORCES
Listen to the hollow booms
As if a gale blows round the rooms.
Dead trees crashing!
Downpour splashing!
Thunder shakes the palace roof... yes thunder!
Yet the moon shines brightly... What a wonder!

KORDIAN *looking into the conference room*
The room is flooded with silvery light,
The crown lies on a golden tripod,
The Czar's crown today, but after this night,
The crown will belong only to God!
Let's go... I can't take my eyes off the crown!

IMAGINATION
Look longer! And see the blood dripping down!
Stooping below it, black as pitch,
A man hard at work...

TERROR
There are horns on his forehead, below which
Lidless eyes shine like fire,
Who is he, why does he lurk?

KORDIAN
Who is he? What's his desire?

PHANTOM
The Czar was wearing this crown.
The blood of Peter, the blood of Ivan,
As from a bowl is pouring down;
I try to clean this Polish floor,
But not a drop can I make gone,
Of all these pools of Royal gore,
For at least a century!...

KORDIAN
If Polish rivers will not wash it clean,
Then bring me blood so that we might
Use that and it will be as white
As a dead man's face.

Kordian

After a moment

I must still pass through one more room.

Enters Throne Room

Black windows and a starless sky, and gloom,
A fiery column shows me where to pace.
The lamp guards Caesar, lights his bed,
And pours out on the glassy floor
Like moonshine on a lake. It sheds
Its fiery waves right through the door
To rock my boat... I'm dizzy... Who is there?

IMAGINATION
Blazing bayonets fly through the air
Converging together, their edges keen,
Like fish in a bowl when they have seen
A scrap of food.
They mesh together and scratch their steel,
Which flash and exude
Sparks that sprinkle down with a squeal.
So wait until the whole hive of flames swarm...

TERROR
Just don't turn around—for there at the door...

KORDIAN turns around

IMAGINATION
In malachite vases, two trees are growing,
Whether it's sunny or whether it's snowing,
Their leaves are human ears, their flowers eyes,
And they should have born fruit with human tongues,[114]
But the Czar plucked them out to strike them dumb...
They stand guard like Haiduks[115] of giant size...

---

114. Allusion to the secret police and the network of spies or informants.
115. Haiduks were Hungarian foot soldiers used in Polish armies in the sixteenth
century Later, doormen in nobles' houses, wearing similar uniforms, were so called.

Watching with flower, listening with leaf;
As silent as the Trappist monks,
Pouring all into their trunks...

KORDIAN
Trees see and hear? Beyond belief!

TERROR
Don't look through the window at the dark street!

KORDIAN looks through the window

IMAGINATION
A funeral procession comes in view,
From church to castle, with candle and sheet,
With many corpses... one, two,
Score upon score upon score...
Thousands, I can't count any more.
Crowns and scepters, royal cloaks, [116]
From the candles bluish smoke
Clouds each corpse's face of bone,
And each corpse his coffin bears,
They pile them up like stone on stone,
Building up a tow'r of stairs,
Right against the palace wall,
So many coffins that they crush;
They have built a tower so tall
Corpses climb, they rush...

KORDIAN
                              Where?

IMAGINATION
                              In here!

KORDIAN
To suffocate the Czar with coffins?

---

116. Kordian's vision here is of the Kings of Poland, coming from the church cellar of
the previous scene in a ghastly procession. Imagination and Terror in this scene are
connected to aspects of Kordian's conscience raised by the Chairman. Kordian is not
free of them, as he had insisted earlier.

Kordian

IMAGINATION
                        Hush!
Look there... A monster with a flaming leer
Comes from the room where the Czar has his bed,
And even though you cannot hear his tread,
The floorboards break beneath his hideous feet.

TERROR
Smell the blood! From the room came he
Where Caesar sleeps beneath white sheets,
From in there!

IMAGINATION
            Did you see?

KORDIAN
                    Did I see?

TERROR
What did he do there?

KORDIAN
                What did he do there?

DEVIL
I tried to choke the Czar, but then, I swear,
He looked just like my father in his sleep... [117]

IMAGINATION
Do you hear the funeral bells groan deep?
On every side the tolling swells...

KORDIAN *in horror*
I here them, yes! I hear the bells—

IMAGINATION
Lightning at the window pane
A corpse has climbed the coffins and he stands
Silent with his candle flame
Wind rips his cloak, a worm on every strand

97

---

117. Lady Macbeth says about King Duncan, "had he not resembled/ My father as he slept, I had done't." *Macbeth* Act II, scene 2 ll. 12–13.

Kordian

Like a thick white thread...
The executioner, to bones devolved,
Enacting what the corpses have resolved...
He pounds the window and it breaks to pieces...

KORDIAN
Holy Mother Mary! My Sweet Jesus!

IMAGINATION
He's disappeared... the coffins fall like thunder.

TERROR
Go back! This is the devil's house! Don't blunder!

KORDIAN
I'll go despite the devil's voice,
To cool myself off with his blood.
A crowd of spirits in a flood
To bar my way... I have no choice
I must get through... They will not part.
Pale, silent phantoms, weak of heart,
Like peacocks with a hundred eyes, [118]
They watch the door behind which lies
The sleeping Czar in his bedroom...
Tell me, do you want to know
The color of his blood? And so,
Why doesn't he wake up? I could consume
The speaking of a hundred thousand souls
And be as silent as a grave...

A bell rings in the dawn

It tolls! It is the morning bell I hear...
A dagger pierces through my ear
And stabs me in the brain!
Jesus! Mary! The pain!

98

---

118. Hundred-eyed Argus was set to watch over Io by Hera. Hermes slew him, but Hera, in honor, had him turned into a peacock.

Kordian

As he speaks these last words he falls senseless in the shape of
a cross upon his bayonet at the door to the Czar's bedchamber.
The Czar comes out of his room with a nightlight in his hand.

CZAR
I heard a thud and dreamed about a storm,
Someone had pressed a sash against my throat. [119]
Felt what my father felt, but felt it longer.
Are dreams always to be the harp of conscience
On which will play the rising gale of fear?
I have to go. Though I may get lost here.

He tries to go out, but bumps into Kordian, lying on the floor.

What's this? What does it mean? Is it a corpse?
Bare bayonet and Polish uniform
From the school for the cadets. He stood guard
But came to kill me? Falling on the threshold…
My brother vouched for them! Behind me, Satan!
Don't let thoughts of my brother interrupt,
You show me my brother in every foe.
It cannot be! Oh, if only this man
Would rise and speak a word! He is still warm…
Get up and speak! Or I will open up
Your throat with my sword! Did my brother send you?

He wounds Kordian in the arm with his sword, and Kordian
opens his eyes.

KORDIAN *in delirium*
At the window there are corpses
Carrying funeral torches.

CZAR
He's come to… Well then open up your mouth,
Was it my brother? Tell me, yes or no!
Was it my brother?

99

---

119. Czar Paul I, Nicholas's father, was strangled with a sash in 1801. Nicholas,
however, born in 1796, could hardly have been involved in the assassination, as is
implied here and in Scene 9.

KORDIAN
As white as a sheet
The Czar is sleeping... Jesus, Mary... Dawn
Is breaking...

CZAR
I can find out nothing from
His words or from his face... It must have been
My brother! Yes! I'm sure it was my brother!

He shouts

My guards! Come in here, Guards!!!

Soldiers rush in. The Czar points at Kordian

Find out if this
Soldier is insane... If not, then shoot him...

100

Scene 6

Insane Asylum. Cells are visible in which sit madmen bound in chains. A few walk about freely. KORDIAN is lying on a cot with a fever. The CARETAKER of the asylum. A foreign DOCTOR.

CARETAKER
You've come to visit our insane asylum?

DOCTOR
Here's authorization.

Gives him a ducat

CARETAKER
Signed with a ducat...
You're free to visit any cell you wish,
Madmen are here, madwomen further on...
I'll lay out the asylum like the pieces
Of a watch. Do you practice medicine?

DOCTOR
Yes.

Kordian

CARETAKER
And what system do you embrace?

DOCTOR
Feeling skulls...

CARETAKER
I see, the system of Gall. [120]

DOCTOR
Yes.

CARETAKER
It might be interesting for you
To ascertain which head of ours is maddest?

DOCTOR
Oh! I can do that using Lavater. [121]

Points to KORDIAN

It's that one!

CARETAKER
Your Aesclepian sight has failed you, [122]
That young man was brought here because the Czar
Thought that he is mad, but the Czar is wrong.
He has a fever but a healthy mind,
It's healthier than yours, even mine.

DOCTOR
Even?

CARETAKER
I see I have offended Gall's disciple!
You would return the favor, burn me back?
Well, if you find that man not right upstairs,
Perhaps you'll find that I'm a madman too?

---

120. Franz Joseph Gall (1758–1828) authored a theory of determining human abilities based on the shape of the skull.
121. Johann K. Lavater (1741–1801) promoted a method of determining a man's character by examining the lines on his face.
122. Aesclepius was a legendary physician of Greek Mythology.

DOCTOR
Who knows? May I smoke a cigar?

CARETAKER
                              I don't
Have a match.

   Throwing down the ducat

                    Damn! The ducat burned my hand.

DOCTOR *picks up the ducat and lights his cigar with it, then gives
it back to the* CARETAKER
Thank you.

CARETAKER
                    My Dear God! This is Satan's work!

DOCTOR
It seems so to you, a rational man,   102
The ducat is as cold as ice, it burns
Because it's red.

CARETAKER
                    Did I imagine this?
Am I really mad? Oh, Virgin Most Holy
Protect me from all evil!

DOCTOR
                              Never look
Upon a ducat with the eyes of reason,
A ducat is an element, primary...

CARETAKER
I see... I must get out of here, for when
I listen to him it just warps my mind.

   Exit CARETAKER

DOCTOR
I chased him out, tomorrow he'll go mad
Thinking about that ducat. Now I hope
That I may speak alone with that young madman.

   He sits on KORDIAN's *bed*

Kordian

KORDIAN

Who are you? My brother? Some blood relation?

DOCTOR

No, I'm just a fellow enthusiast.

KORDIAN

Then I guess you were only born this morning?
For they all tell me I'm the only one.

DOCTOR

Well, you they know; they haven't met me yet.
For I sat silent, hidden in a dagger.

KORDIAN

Give me something to drink... I have a fever...
I cannot understand your words.

DOCTOR

                              Then pay
Attention! I'll explain it clear enough!
But you must pay attention! Strict attention!

KORDIAN

I've paid attention... Now I recognize you...

DOCTOR

I came out of the Czar's bedroom at midnight. [123]

KORDIAN

What did you do in there?

DOCTOR

                    I didn't do
A thing! Just watered some flowers...

KORDIAN

                              Those trees
With eyes and ears, but without tongues?

---

123. The Doctor identifies himself as the Devil of the previous scene who came out of the Czar's bedchamber paraphrasing Shakespeare.

Kordian

DOCTOR

They're maples...
Others have cross-shaped leaves, like cloves. Still others
Are like bent reeds, with twists and turns, but hollow.
The sons of Czars must learn to play these twisty
Hollow reeds. [124]

KORDIAN

Why does your voice echo so?
Try to speak softly... Do you know a prayer?

DOCTOR

Just the one men sing before a battle.

KORDIAN

Not that one... It will be too loud, and Godless...

DOCTOR

It's a Turkish prayer, two-horned like the moon,
One horn kills the enemy, one yourself...

KORDIAN

But don't we have to kill our enemies?

DOCTOR

I know all about this necessity...
A nation dies, and why? So that the bard
Of this nation will have material
For his poems; the bard pours out his rhymes,
That in his song an angel may unearth
A little spark of fire amid the ice
And sing his song in heaven. So you see
How little I value this tribe of bards
Who hold such sway among the masses.

KORDIAN

No!
The other way... From heaven down to earth.

---

124. As mentioned in the notes to Scene 5, the plants now identified as "maples"
represent spies. Those with "cross-shaped leaves" are the many underlings wearing
various decorations, and the "bent reeds" are the bootlickers.

Kordian

DOCTOR
I see. The angel's hymn flows into him.
The nation dies because the poet sings.

KORDIAN
Don't talk inanities! Recite something
From the Old Testament.

DOCTOR
                          When Pharaoh was
At the zenith of his pow'r, he dreamt that
Seven fat cows ate seven skinny ones. [125]

KORDIAN
No, No! It doesn't go like that...

DOCTOR
                          Oh, yes,
Just ask the race of Moguls... [126]

KORDIAN
                          Speak about
Something else. Scripture isn't working.
Are you a botanist?

DOCTOR
                  Keep it a secret,
But I've discovered a new type of plant;
It grows in my window, in a knight's visor,
Sown in cold ash from a hundred old cities.
It should shortly produce a bud as large
As the ideas of a million people,

---

125. The Doctor inverts Pharaoh's dream, which Joseph is called to interpret in Genesis 41, and gives it an entirely new significance. He echoes the common Enlightenment notion that superior force will win out and the strong will take advantage of the weak. The Fables of the Polish Enlightenment poet, Ignacy Krasicki, often express similar sentiment. The devil's expressing Enlightenment and scientific notions further develops a theme begun in the "Preparation" section.
126. The Moguls were the followers of Baber who conquered India in 1526 and founded a Moslem Empire that lasted until 1857. The term is commonly used to represent the rich and powerful. Like Alexander the Great and Napoleon, the Czar had a desire to conquer India, and thus this is another expression of his ambition.

A beautiful flower as red as blood,
And seeds in great pods, which burst with a bang
As from a million cannon... Fascinated?
Your eyes are blazing with poetic flare. [127]

KORDIAN
Is it blooming? Is it spreading?

DOCTOR
                    It sprouts.

KORDIAN
                              Just sprouting?

DOCTOR
Yes, but frost has threatened it.
And so I hid it in a kitchen pot.

KORDIAN
You wear me, break me, gnaw me, make me tremble...
Don't talk of flowers any more... I'm sleepy...

DOCTOR
Three elements comprise the human mind
Three main ingredients. Through them we can
Explain the Holy Trinity most clearly.
The first ingredient is unity,
And from this concept numbers have been born,
The second is infinity, from which
There flows the concept of a boundary.
Third is the notion of comparison;
It is the union of the two, and thus
A trinity is formed of all of them;
Without numbers, unity would not stand,
Without boundaries, infinity fades;
So one is equal to the other, like

127. The Doctor's poetic imagery foreshadows the coming Insurrection.

Kordian

The Father to the Son, comparison
Gives life, the Holy Spirit, and all three
Ideas form a trinity—Reason. [128]

KORDIAN
The roaring of the ocean fills my ears,
I'm feverish... What are you saying, damn it?

DOCTOR
I'm curing you... Now on to the creation of
The world, or rather of the peoples in it...
People have taken the place of the world;
The earth's a nut enclosed in hull of clouds.
In six days God created the earth's peoples.
On the first day, He created the praying
Nation of Judah, and this was the earth
And the other nations grew upon it.
Day two he poured the Eastern peoples: water;
Day three he planted Greek tribes as the trees;
Day four the sun of Socrates shone high;
Day five he let the Roman eagles fly,
And these became the birds, but at the end
There came the gloomy night of Middle Ages.
On the sixth he made a man, Napoleon. [129]
This is day seven, God puts down his hands
And rests after his work, creating no one.

KORDIAN
You lie, vile one! Each man who's dedicated
To Freedom is God's newest handiwork.

DOCTOR
Ha! Freedom turns the potter's wheel today,
You speak the truth, the wheel's on a new track,
It will produce a pot made out of clay.

---

128. This is a paraphrase of the ideas presented in Victor Cousin's
Cours de Philosophie lesson 5 (1818)
129. This representation of the periodization of history is most popularly represented
by Hegel, but it has its origin in the philosophy of Johann Gottfried Herder (1744–
1803). The passage reflects a belief that the end of history had arrived.

Kordian

KORDIAN
It will produce great men!

DOCTOR
                    Well no, you see?
The fever has subsided in your brain,
You speak entirely to the point...

KORDIAN
                       Then, listen,
Now tell me honestly if you have seen
A man or angel who has offered up
His suffering to men in sacrifice?
Who offers up his head as target for
The falling thunderbolts and suffers death
For all in imitation of our Savior...

DOCTOR
Such men came with me, I will summon them.

*He calls to two madmen, one holds his arms straight out to
his sides in the shape of a cross, the other has one hand raised
to the air.*

Both of these men have suffered for all people,
They'll tell you how they suffered; you can judge...

To the MADMAN with arms stretched out into a cross

Tell me, brother, what sort of man are you?[130]

---

130. In presenting these two madmen, the Doctor skeptically attacks the views
of man's purpose put forward by the Christian and Enlightenment viewpoints
respectively. The former is that man should imitate Christ, offering himself up as
a sacrifice for mankind. The second is the use of reason to understand the world,
and to view the world as a great chain of nature, in which man is the vital link.
This play presents a clear example of the way in which Modernist ideas were born
in the late Romanticism. The Romantic movement is often seen as a revolt against
the rationalism and empiricism of the Enlightenment. However, late Romanticism
turned quite bitter, for it began to realize that the spiritual values held before the
Enlightenment could not be returned to, and new spiritual values invented by
Romantic philosophers fell short of providing satisfying answers. The suspicion that
the world is neither rational nor divine, and is merely a chaotic abyss, is played on by
the devil. This motif of the abyss is first brought up in the "Preparation" section.

Kordian

FIRST MADMAN
I'm not a man; a long, long time ago
I was changed into a tree
The cross of Jesus' suffering and woe,
They pounded that man onto me,
I held him in my arms, not with the nails,
Just like a baby when he wails.
I am the cross! And if the Pope should give
Out pieces of the cross, do not believe!
I have my arms and legs, I'm whole, I live!

Speaking sadly as he exits

Lord, take away this bitter cup, relieve
Me!

DOCTOR
　　Look, he's sacrificed for men.

KORDIAN
　　　　　　　　He's mad!

DOCTOR *to the* MADMAN *with his arm in the air*
And why is your arm in the air, my lad?

SECOND MADMAN
Speak softly! I protect the world,
By holding up the azure ceiling of
The heavens with this hand held high above.
The sky, the sun, the moon would like to hurl
Themselves on everybody's head! I stand
Beneath the sloping roof of heaven, I stay
Awake, but I am tired and sad. So pray
To me as I protect you and this land
From heaven's flood: the everyday redeemer.
Go to sleep my people! Good night, sweet dreamers.

Exit

DOCTOR
Great man! He's sacrificed himself for all!

Kordian

KORDIAN
A madman!

DOCTOR
         Is that blasphemy that's flung
From your oral catapult?

KORDIAN
              They're both mad!
You must have driven them insane yourself!

DOCTOR
How do you know you're not as mad as they?
You wished to kill a phantom, sacrifice
For nothing. Goldfish in a crystal bowl
Pound against the hard but unseen borders.
This crystal sphere of air in which you splash,
This world is an abyss of nothingness.

KORDIAN
I think.

DOCTOR
      And so the world's your thought.

KORDIAN
                I suffer.

DOCTOR
Stop thinking!

KORDIAN
      But I can't...

DOCTOR
          Oh yes, you can.
Just think of ways to stop yourself from thinking.
Go mad and be a saint in Istanbul. [131]

---

131. A return to the Dervish motif from the Prologue.

KORDIAN
You came here to suck the soul from my soul,
You Satan! You have stolen my last treasure,
My conviction, extinguished my last gleam.

DOCTOR
I've crushed the Divine clay...

KORDIAN
                Merciful God,
Deliver me from this wretched creature's talons!

> *GRAND DUKE CONSTANTINE comes in with soldiers and points at Kordian*

GRAND DUKE
Seize him! Take him to be tortured and die!

KORDIAN
Human voices! You saved me after all,
Oh Lord! Although you freed me from this man
Into the arms of death.

> *Points to the place from which the DOCTOR has disappeared*

          Where did he go?

GRAND DUKE
As soon as he has on his uniform
Take him to Saxon Square... [132]

> *Exit*

KORDIAN
          Where did he go?

SOLDIER
Hurry up, come on, the Grand Duke is waiting.

111

---

132. The site of military parades in Warsaw.

Kordian

Scene 7

*Saxon Square. The Polish Army, not yet completely assembled...
A group of generals on one side, among them the* CZAR, *and the*
GRAND DUKE CONSTANTINE *who is pacing nervously back and
forth... In the background, all around the square are the people
of Warsaw.*

CHORUS
Thousands of bayonets, thousands of soldiers,
Banners hang limp, bayonets don't tremble,
As quiet as the Last Judgment.

GRAND DUKE *in command*
To the front! Order at the front!

CHORUS
The infantry closed ranks in one long row.
If the Czar would stand out by just one inch
And on the other side was William Tell,
An arrow could graze every Polish chest
And strike the Adam's apple of the Czar. [133]

GRAND DUKE
Play!

CHORUS
    Janissary music was thundering, [134]
But now the music's stopped... The Czar will speak...

CZAR *to the soldiers*
Are you well, my lads?

---

133. Saxon Square had been chosen by the conspirators as the site of the assassination
of the Czar. The reference is not only to William Tell's famous act of shooting an
apple off his son's head, but also to his stature as a patriot.
134. The Janissaries were Christian prisoners of war forced to serve in the Turkish
army. The reference is not only to the loud, military music that had been playing on
the square, but also to the Polish soldiers, forced to serve the Czar.

VOICE OF THE SOLDIERS
> Yes! Thanks be to God!

CHORUS
What they say in that din God alone understands,
Like a prayer that's smashed by the roar of the sea.

> *Six soldiers lead the pale* KORDIAN *forward. They place him in*
> *front of the* CZAR... *The* GRAND DUKE *runs up in a rage.*

GRAND DUKE *foaming at the mouth. To* KORDIAN.
You're here, you Polish Dog! But why so pale?
Have you foreseen what's coming? Raskolnik![135]
You still wear epaulettes? I'll rip them off!
I'll brush away those bugs! Then I'll throw you
Underneath the hooves of these three columns,
Or bury your body here in the sand,
And write the word "*VOR*" on your brow with my spur.[136]
The Czar gave you to me for my revenge...
The Czar himself has dug your grave! No Devil
Can ever release you from my tight grasp!

CZAR *aside*
Who does he think he's fooling?[137]

GRAND DUKE
> Bring four horses!
You have a fever? But your body's whole!
You dog! We'll leave a limb on each nag's tail,
My strongest horse will rip your head right off.
Silent? I'll turn rabid! The dog is silent!

> *Punches* KORDIAN *in the chest with his fist*

---

135. The Raskolniki were the old believer schismatics who were persecuted by Ivan
the Terrible. The term is used figuratively for renegades.

136. Vor means "thief" in Russian. Felons were sometimes branded with this word on
their forehead in Czarist Russia.

137. The Czar still believes that his brother, Grand Duke Constantine, put Kordian
up to the assassination attempt.

I'm hungry for your body like a wolf!

Gnashes his teeth

Ha! Czar, do you like equestrian sports?
I'll show you a jump... Pile your rifles up
Into a pyramid, tie them together
Like sheaves, with their bayonets in the air.

The soldiers set up this pyramid of rifles

Now sit on a horse, you dog, and then fly
With him to Hell. Are you still silent? What?
Has the sight of these rifles made you weak?
And do you think that I might show some mercy?
I'm sacrificing my horse, do you hear?
I've sacrificed my horse! And what of you?
Now go! Go on! I wish that I could pick
You up in an elephant's trunk and throw
You on those thorns! I'd throw you there myself...

Calms down

Don't shame me now, Polak, listen to me...
I told the Czar that all the Poles are madmen,
Ready to jump from here to the Vistula... [138]

Enraged

So jump! Or I will have you stuffed into
The catacombs of Carmelites. [139] I'll have
You starved to death! Locked up with skeletons!

In a pleading tone

If you survive the bayonets, I'll give
You back your life...

138. The river running through Warsaw.
139. The former Carmelite monastery in Warsaw was used as a prison for political offenders.

KORDIAN
                    Thank you, Grand Duke, thank you
For clarifying everything... If I
Could win the gift of life by moving just
One finger, that finger would never move!

GRAND DUKE
The scoundrel is afraid!

CZAR
                    If that is your
Concern, I'll put your mind at rest. I swear
That even if you do escape unharmed
And like a bird you clear the bayonets,
You'll not escape a bullet in your brain!
You are correct, Grand Duke, he is afraid!

GRAND DUKE
You see, the Czar has said it... You will die...
My soldiers! I will give a St. Anne's Cross
To anyone who'll jump. St. Stanislas[140]
If you are wounded... Add a pension of
A thousand zloty... Make it two thousand...
Four thousand... Oh, you dogs! You rabbits! Poles!!!

KORDIAN
Bring me the horse!

He mounts the horse and rides to the edge of the square

GRAND DUKE *calls to GENERAL KURUTA[141]*
                    Come over here, Kuruta!
I hope he makes it!

GENERAL KURUTA
                    He deserves the knout!

115

---

140. St. Anne's Cross and St. Stalinislas' are both military decorations.
141. General Dmitri Kuruta, Grand Duke Constantine's chief of staff.

GRAND DUKE
I want him to make it! Let him make it!
The Czar will see my soldiers fly above
The Muscovites... Look there, he rides... He stops...
He's looking over there... Right at the crowd...
The crowd is standing quiet, muddy, black.

Scowls like a tiger

I do not like these people... Look, they're waving
Their handkerchiefs and throwing up their caps...
Kuruta! Is there any hope? Please, Lord...

KURUTA
I share your hope, Your Excellency, yes...

GRAND DUKE *heatedly*
Look, look, there's nothing but a cloud of dust!
Can't see... Spur your horse! Ha! He's jumped...

ARMY *shouts*

Hurrah!

PEOPLE *cry in the distance*
He lives!

Soldiers lead the reeling KORDIAN. *The* GRAND DUKE *grabs him
in an embrace.*

GRAND DUKE
What's wrong with you, my friend! Well, well!
Brave lad! My horse was not bad either, eh?
He jumps as if possessed or mad. Your Highness
Did you see it? Take my horse off to rest.

To KORDIAN

I'll intercede for you. Go! Are you ill?
Sleepy? Take him away. Put him to bed...

They lead KORDIAN *away*

CZAR *to the generals, so that the* GRAND DUKE *cannot hear*
He threatened my life. Arrange a court martial,
Have him shot...

Kordian

GRAND DUKE

       Trumpeters! Play the Dąbrowski
Mazurka,[142] the Grand Duke, himself, will dance it...

Scene 8

Parade on Saxon Square. A monk's cell being used as a prison.
Bars on the windows, a wooden table and bed. KORDIAN,
condemned to death, is talking with a cloistered priest. The
old servant, GRZEGORZ, *walks around the room with tears*
in his eyes.

GRZEGORZ

That priest has tortured my master an hour
Already. Why can't they leave him alone
Before his death? What sort of God would say:
"Lock the child in prison"? There is no God,
I'll side with Satan...

KORDIAN

       Gregorz, pray for me!

GRZEGORZ falls on his knees and prays like a scolded child...
KORDIAN *kneels at the foot of the priest, who blesses him and*
makes him rise, saying:

PRIEST

My son! Rise from the ashes; fly to God,
Forgive the world. God will deliver you
Out of the lion's mouth and from this dungeon,
Where you would wilt just like a faded flower...
Before your journey to eternity,
What will you leave to those left here on earth?

---

142. "Jeszcze Polska nie zginęła," which now serves as the Polish National Anthem. It was named for General Jan Henryk Dąbrowski (1755–1818), hero of the Kościuszko Insurrection who later organized and commanded the Polish legions in Napoleon's army. In 1814 he was one of the generals entrusted by Czar Alexander I with the reorganization of the Polish Army.

Kordian

KORDIAN
Nothing.

PRIEST
    To no one on earth?

KORDIAN
        No one here.

PRIEST
Is there no one you call friend?

KORDIAN
        No one, no.

PRIEST
That's a sin you did not confess to me!
Have mercy on him, Mighty Lord, Our God!

KORDIAN
Before I give my body to the ground,
I hear a voice that echoes in my soul;
It calls for memory, some trace on earth...

PRIEST
That is a sin, my son... You youngsters want
To leave a lasting mark when you depart
This world, incite a thought or bloody sword;
Wherefore this passion? Honest farmers do
Not gather dead and fallen leaves, nor do
These help the soul like prayers on the lips
Of the departing... Sorry! I've depressed you...
I am too old, and you a child of spring...
I did not understand... Listen, near
The monastery lies a garden shaded
By rows of pines... I'll plant a china rose
In your name there today. And it will blossom
Despite the cold with flowers that are pale
And melancholy...

Kordian

KORDIAN

                    May the Lord grant you
A stream of comfort! Planted in my name?
Perhaps they will not wither?

   Exit PRIEST

                       Let all dreams
Stop flying aimlessly and come together
In one great cloud of thoughts and be with me!
Oh, heaven! Light the sun and moon and stars
For me as I lay dying! There, before
The people, though impaled upon a stake,
I will hold in my suffering and conquer
My pain, but here my pride won't stop my tears...
If only I were sure that I could bid
Farewell to this world and never return!
At the moment of my departure, I
Would look at the earth with different eyes,
More interested and perhaps with tears...
Amid a flower garden, there might be
A brand new flower... And I wouldn't know!...
A string might give a new sound, and I would
Not hear it. And yet, something troubles me!
I would not like to know the people, but
I would like to acquaint myself with earth,
The nursemaid of the people! Oh, my Earth!
Have you been a faithful nursemaid to me?

   After a moment, with disdain

Then let the vile masses gather in swarms
And spit on their dead mother. I will not
Be with them! Let these human couples bear
New types of beings, opposite of human,
Let them turn the world inside out and show
The evil side of righteousness. Until
The world, just like an image that's reversed
In a glass, will return into the womb

Of God, no longer like the Lord's creation. [143]
Let those Liliputians, tiny as ants,
Profess themselves to be the people! I
Will not be with them! —The word MOTHERLAND
Will shrink to the four letters that spell CZAR;
Let Love, and Faith, and all the language of
The people sink into this single word
I will not be with them! Let gallows grow
In city gardens, lining all the lanes,
And let the crowd walk down these lanes with smiles
Of friendship and with tears of hatred in
Their eyes. Let nursemaids walk the children through
These gardens filled with leafless gallows trees,
To play by digging in the sand, that's red
With martyr's blood... I will not be with them!
Oh, Dead Poles! I am coming to join you!
I am the wage-earner, whom Christ did not
Refrain from paying, even though he was
The last to plant the grapes; the payment is
A dark and quiet grave, as you were paid... [144]

GRZEGORZ
Oh, Lord! I cannot finish up the prayer
That says "forgive those who trespass against us."
I hope that God will punish them on earth!
My dear young Master, oh, why did you place
That pistol up against your pale, white forehead?
I still remember how the moon's eye shone,
And someone kept calling my name... "Grzegorz!"
In the woods—Suddenly I saw my child
Amid the bushes; red blood flowed, like rubies...

KORDIAN
Don't remind me of that!

---

143. This passage stands in opposition to the optimistic view of the world which will follow a divine plan to become more perfect.
144. Allusion to the parable of the laborers in the vineyard, Matthew 20.

Kordian

GRZEGORZ

You marked your brow
With Satan's seal, and now you're going to die.
You see... A man should love himself more than
His brother: if God punished Cain for killing[145]
His brother, why then everyone who tries
To put a bullet in his head or poisons...

He stops in mid-sentence, then continues in despair

I could foresee misfortune, but not this—
Death at the hands of an executioner!!!
Oh, dear Master! Comfort me! Talk to me!
I'll get a scribe to take down all your words,
Old Gregorz will keep them against his breast,
I'll have my children plant them in my grave
For children's words are flowers to the old...

KORDIAN
Do you have children?

GRZEGORZ

Yes, I have a son...

KORDIAN
And is he married?

GRZEGORZ nods his head

If a son is born
To your son, have him Christened with my name,
Kordian...

GRZEGORZ

Oh Master, I would have to cry
Each time I called my grandson "Kordian!"

KORDIAN
Don't call him that! The name will injure him...
No, do not name him Kordian!

---

145. The wound of Kordian's attempted suicide is compared to the mark which God
placed on Cain for murdering Abel, his brother. Genesis 4:15.

Kordian

GRZEGORZ

                    My young lord!
Do not take back what you have given me;
Already I'm accustomed to the thought:
My little one, although a beggar, poor...
Will have the name of "Kordian"... And if he
Is mischievous, I'll never punish him.
I'll let him grow up wild, just like a flower,
My little Kordian! My tiny cornflower!

    Laughs, with tears in his eyes

Oh, Master! Master! You will never see him!

KORDIAN

My God! Would you really punish a child
With my name, or make his life like my life?
It's strange how a man drowning in despair
Will clutch at every straw, seek to live on...

    Pensive

Well then, after they take away my life,
Long after this old man has buried me,
The voice of a young mother will cry out,
"Oh, Kordian!" after her wandering child,
The voice will linger in the groves and meadows...
The child will answer, laughing mid the flowers...
Meanwhile, amid dark clouds, within a cloister
My rose will bloom... A priest that's robed in black
Will say a pray'r for me... And so that's it...
My legacy: a rose and one small child.

    Enter an OFFICER *with the* PRIEST, *in tears*

PRIEST
My son!

KORDIAN
        How will death come?

OFFICER
>   By firing squad...

GRZEGORZ falls to his knees. KORDIAN *takes his grey head in both hands and kisses it, saying, in a broken voice*

KORDIAN
Farewell, father, my faithful one...
Exit

GRZEGORZ *stretching out his arms*
>   Lord! Master!

He falls on the ground... Then he gets up and runs out after KORDIAN

Scene 9

A room in the Royal Palace.

123

CZAR *alone*
I'm bored! Too bad I fired that chamberlain
Who used to dance for me on two hind paws
Like a pug-dog, hop, hop. I'd like to get
That Sultan Mahmud to hop before me... [146]
I would treat him to sulfur and gunpowder
Until I had choked him in all the smoke...

Looks at the wall

What's this? There's filth and dust on all these walls?
There in the corners spider webs trap flies.
Dust... dust... This dust amuses me, it shows
This building to be desolate. It is
A weed on the grave of my enemy...
Poland has already turned cold... She's dead...
A compass needle turned forever north,
Always watching frozen Siberia.

---

146. Mahmud II, Sultan of Turkey, with whom the Czar was waging war (1827–1829).

Kordian

The corpse of this country seems threatening
From a distance, often it has disturbed
My dreams of conquest... But when I came here
The corpse shook, even smiled... I saw no tears...
Didn't they carpet the houses with flowers?
So onward... Europe has been cut in pieces
Just like an apple, but the poisoned knife
Has poisoned both halves. Kings! Bow before me!
And doff your crowns in sign of fealty!
Ha! Am I great or is this world so small?
Is the world stupid, or am I so wise?
The proud Shah gave me part of his huge country; [147]
I had some of his sand burned into glass,
The Shah received a crystal bed, and thanked me.
Oh, Brother of the Moon, Son of the Sun!
Isn't the Czar's glass bed too cold for you?
A hundred headed monster has arisen
In the West, so I'll order another
Bed from the foundry in St. Petersburg,
For the nations of the West. And the length
Will fit the Moscow race exactly, and
If a nation is too long for the bed,
I will not stretch the glass, but shorten them
By a head. [148] Hear me, peoples of the world!
I'm sending you a crystal bed!... Who's that?
My Brother!

GRAND DUKE CONSTANTINE runs in out of breath

How are you, Kostya! What's new?

---

147. "Fath 'Ali Shah (ruled 1791–1834), in need of revenue, relied on British subsidies but lost the Caucasus to Russia by the treaties of Golestan in 1813 and Turkmanchay in 1828. The last gave Russian commercial and consular agents entrance to Iran, and this began a diplomatic rivalry between Russia and Britain that victimized Iran." "Iran" *The New Encyclopaedia Britannica* 15th edition, vol. 21.

148. The classical allusion is to Procrustes of Greek mythology, who had such a bed and forced passers-by to sleep in it. Theseus killed him as one of his labors. The historical allusion is to the Czar's project for intervention in France during the July Revolution.

GRAND DUKE
Imperial Majesty...

CZAR
     Can't you breathe?
I see you ran here. Why in such a hurry?
You must have come with some good news for me.

GRAND DUKE
Well... Your Imperial Majesty... You...
Gave orders...

CZAR
    Speak boldly!

GRAND DUKE
       To have him shot...

CZAR
Such was my pleasure, my dear Brother...

GRAND DUKE
         Please...
Recant, Your Imperial Majesty!
Take back your sentence of death.

CZAR
       But, Grand Duke,
What does this mean?

GRAND DUKE
      Oh please, let this man live
Imperial Majesty! Let us not
Lose time... not even a blink of an eye.
Here's a reprieve, a pen...

CZAR
      I used my pen
To write a death sentence; I stand by it.

GRAND DUKE
Your Majesty, put a mark on the paper,
 A signature... For God's sake...

Kordian

CZAR

Brother dear,
Tell me the truth. You want to save this man?
This Kordian?

GRAND DUKE

Yes, I do! I do! I do!

CZAR

Then that's exactly why he has to die.

GRAND DUKE

In shock
What's that? Why?

CZAR

Brother, let us end this quarrel!
I want to sleep...

The GRAND DUKE paces around the room, a storm of anger within his soul... He takes a tile from the stove[149] and crushes it in his hand.

GRAND DUKE

Why won't Your Imperial Majesty
Do just this one little favor for me?
For, after all, I've given you the throne!... [150]

---

149. Tile heating stoves are still used extensively in Poland. Those in the Royal Palace were works of art.

150. In 1822 Constantine renounced his right to the succession of the Czardom after Alexander I in favor of Nicholas, his younger brother. This was not made public until after Alexander's death, and it led to confusion over the succession and to the Decembrist revolt. Although Constantine had no part in that revolt, it had become a sore point between the two brothers, and the present quarrel is a kind of continuation of that conflict. Constantine had been viceroy of Poland since 1815. The essence of their quarrel is political. Nicholas wants to rule as an absolute monarch. Constantine wants to rule Poland independently and wishes to preserve constitutional independence for Poland as promised by Alexander. Constantine, who was married to a Polish woman, respected Polish national customs. He is also eager to have the trust of the Polish army, which he commands. This helps to explain why he is so eager to save Kordian.

CZAR
My Brother, you had better stop this anger;
Stop flaring your nostrils.

GRAND DUKE
                                        Please forgive me,
Your Majesty! I'll stop. But let him live!

CZAR
If he is not a murderer, then you are...
Leave me, dear Brother. I don't want to look
Into the filth inside your heart; I would
Prefer to dig up graves for two whole months.

GRAND DUKE
What? I don't understand?

CZAR
                                        Just go away,
Leave me alone.

GRAND DUKE
                                My Brother, you had better
Not try to grab a tiger by the tail!
I've given you the throne on which you sit!
I lie before it like a lion made
Of bronze. And what if I should roar? Won't people
Then know that I'm alive? Won't they remember
Then that it should be me upon the throne?
And you back in the stable... drilling troops?

CZAR
Grand Duke! I see you've overfilled your cup!
What is it you said? You gave me the throne?
It was there for the taking, my dear Brother!
Into a purple chamber you were born,
A hundred cannons rocked your golden cradle,
They Christened you for the Greek Emperor;[151]
But later, your mother, wife of Czar Paul,

---

151. The Czar of Russia was considered the successor to the Roman Emperor and thus also of the Byzantine Emperor.

Began to loathe you, you degenerate!
You had a Tatar nose... Instead of sucking
You bit your mother's breast, just like a puppy...
When you grew up, your mother called you, "Moron,"
And your own conscience told you it was so.
She said to you, "Give your brother the throne!"
You answered, "Let my brother buy it!" So
The abdication of the throne was bought.
It was there for the taking. What advantage
Would you have gotten from it? Could you look
Into your mother's eyes and face her as
The Czar? And could you face her smirking mouth with
The words, "You Moron," written on her lips?
And would you drink a goblet that was filled
By those old wrinkled hands of your dear mother?[152]

GRAND DUKE

Czar! Czar! You kept the poison until last.
I knew you very well, you proud and shameless
Executioners! Mother taught you how
To kill with words. Just two of us were clever,
The third was stupid; when somebody told
The smart ones, "We'll strangle your father with
A sash." They answered, "Good!" And it was done...[153]
Don't you remember, when Benningsen came[154]
And said, "We strangled Czar Paul," they replied:
"Amen..." So it was they that killed their father.
They blamed the sash and only it was punished.
They threw the sash beyond the Moscow borders
Into the country of her neighbors, thus
They gave a nest of yellow snakes to Europe.

---

152. Słowacki continues his allusions to the Roman Empire, suggesting especially the poisoning activities of Livia, the wife of Augustus.

153. As mentioned above, Nicholas was only five at the time of his father's assassination.

154. Leonty Bennigsen (1745–1826) played an active role in the conspiracy that led to Paul's assassination and was subsequently made governor-general of Lithuania by Alexander.

And after the priest whispered one quick prayer,
They threw the blessed body of their father
Into a dungeon. Why did you not carry
His body out upon his golden throne?
Because the murderers had left him crumpled,
Like a slain leopard with black and blue spots.
The nation shouted, "Sons, you've robbed us of
The spectacle of a state funeral,
The tears of princes, and the pleasant sight
Of kings laid low... Bring out your father's body!
Kiss his hands! For we want to see ourselves
What kind of Czars these are that kill
Without a judge or sentence!" You remember,
How, choked with incense smoke, you kissed his hands,
And the funeral kiss upon his mouth?
All the water of the Neva[155] was not
Enough to wash your mouth off after that.
Brother, oh how much you look like our father...
I can't look at you! Wash your face! Wash off
The similarity... I cannot look
At you... Or else I will utter a curse,
And when God hears...

CZAR

It was a crime for kings.

GRAND DUKE

And what of those you punish every day
By sending them off to Siberia?
They'll cry from their kibitkas,[156] "You are one
Of us, Oh Czar! So come and ride with us!
You killed your father, so now you must allow
The executioner to kiss you forehead
With his red-hot branding iron..." But you
Have kept the people ignorant without

---

155. The main river of St. Petersburg.
156. Kibitkas were long, covered wagons or sleighs used, among other things, to take prisoners to Siberia.

Kordian

Access to education. A few voices
Were raised from the Imperial Guards' ranks;
So send them up against the Turks! "You lead
Them, Michael..." But he didn't have a plan...
"Know what to do?" He didn't understand.
"Plant mines beneath the ranks, you idiot!"
You shouted, "Then explode them!" Michael saluted—
Then bowed in silence and went out—a month
Later the mines beneath the guards exploded
Like a thunderbolt—the ground was soaked through
With Russian blood...[157] The Czar just smiled and said
It was a terrible mistake! But you
Know what, My Czar? The knout and even exile
Would not be punishment enough for that!
Penal servitude would not be enough!...

CZAR
Even a hired assassin would be put
To shame by your black heart, my dearest Brother.
Shall I remind you of that incident?

GRAND DUKE
What incident?

CZAR
           I never lie. You know!

He whispers a few words into the GRAND DUKE's ear

GRAND DUKE
No, my Czar! Be silent! Please, do not speak...

CZAR
No, not until I've whipped you with my words,
Until I penetrate your head and bake
Your brain!

GRAND DUKE
          You will enrage me, Czar! Be silent!

157. Michael, younger brother of Nicholas, fought in the Russian war with Turkey (1827–1829) and there took part in the described massacre of the Imperial Guards.

CZAR
Be silent?... I am not the conscience of
The Grand Duke, nor am I his hired flunky...

GRAND DUKE
A thousand curses on you, please be silent!

CZAR
What became of that pretty English girl?[158]
Sixteen years old and shy, with snow-white skin,
And sky blue eyes, the belle of all the balls,
Sometimes happy, sometimes sad, frail but lively—
So naive of emotions and the world
That she could be in love with a white rose,
And hide behind the curtain of her bed
Embarrassed by the stare of blooming roses...

The GRAND DUKE sits down and stares fixedly at the wall

The hand of God had sprinkled all his diamonds
On her as well as fire from all his stars...
This fragile crystal creature could not bend—
And so she shattered—How appropriate...

GRAND DUKE
Yes, I can see her now...

CZAR
                         And then one day
A royal carriage stopped before her house;
Lackeys invited her to the Queen's ball.
As flighty as a butterfly, she went
In a light gown; they led her to the castle—
Into an unknown bedroom. She then asked
Where is the ball? The music, flow'rs and lights?
But everything was silent. They led her...
But you know where they led her... You had not
Yet wiped her spittle off your face. Vindictive
You shouted out... And an entire unit
Of furious soldiers rushed in... She fainted...

---

158. This is based on an authentic incident from Constantine's youth.

GRAND DUKE
Don't finish, Czar, or I'll tear out your tongue!

CZAR
Sit down and listen, for I know the end
Of this amusing story. As a joke
The lover killed the girl; but how to hide
The body? Couldn't bury it in snow,
For it was summer. But he had to hide
Her from the Czar, and also from the envoy
From whom the prince had stolen her, but where?
One of the prince's friends was pressed to service,
He dyed his hair and then disguised his face,
Then, faithful as Pylades, [159] wore rich clothes
And crosses, played the role of Count. He rented
Half a house, and paid for it in advance.
He moved a massive cupboard with his things;
I wonder what was in it? "Women's gowns!"
The porter's daughters thought. Dependable
Pylades locked the door and disappeared.
A week went by, then two… Then secret whispers…
The porter looked in through a crack, saw no one…
But suddenly he shouted: "Stench, the stench!"
So he broke down the door and forced the lock
That sealed the cupboard… Something terrible
Hit every sense at once; a skeleton,
And decomposing human flesh turned liquid…
A gem forgotten flashed upon the corpse.
That ring talked and spoke two names: yours and hers.

GRAND DUKE *rouses himself from a deep stupor and speaks in a muffled*
scream, jumping from his chair
You're calling me a murderer, My Czar?
I'll shove those very words right down your throat!
Can you stomach the secret you have swallowed?
You think I used a sword to pierce her heart?
Perhaps I will rip out your heart as well!

132

---

159. Pylades was Orestes's faithful friend and the archetype of such fidelity.

Perhaps I shot her in the head? Well then
I might decorate the walls with your brains!
If I should flash my sword here at the window,
I'd call some forty thousand bayonets.
But why? I'll knock you down and strangle you,
I'll lock you in the royal cupboard, then
I'll go out happy to the Warsaw streets.
Ha, Ha, Ha, Ha! I'll call a crowd together...
They'll ask me: Where's your brother? Where's the Czar?
I'll answer: "In the cupboard!" Ha, ha, ha!
I locked the Czar up like the naked sword
Of an executioner, in a scabbard
Of putrefaction! Now there let him rust!
Let the people smell the air! Are you trembling,
My Brother? I'm as strong as any tiger...
You know that we're alone here in this room...
So what will it be? Look me in the eye!   133

> *The CZAR looks into his brother's eyes... They stare at one another*
> *for a long time, trying to stare each other down... Constantine*
> *is the first to look away... and backs down... He paces about the*
> *room... The CZAR watches all his movements and says to himself:*

CZAR
That's good! I got out of that in one piece...
That Moscow snake could never start a riot...
He only kills with words... But if instead
He used his sword, then I'd be dead already...
He's lost in thought... He strikes his furrowed brow;
I must anticipate him...

Aloud

Constantine!

GRAND DUKE
Take my sword, Imperial Majesty...

CZAR
I forgive you, Brother!

Kordian

CONSTANTINE stands in silence with his head bowed low.
The CZAR takes his sword, then signs KORDIAN's reprieve, and,
sticking it onto the end of the sword, hands them both to the
GRAND DUKE, saying:

Take back your sword,

And take this with it.

The GRAND DUKE nods his head—takes the sword, then rings
vigorously. The Adjutant enters... The GRAND DUKE gives him
the reprieve.

GRAND DUKE
Take my horse and fly

To the Campus Martius,[160] beat him, gallop,
And heaven help you if a single hair
On Kordian's head is harmed before you get there.

134

Exit Adjutant

CZAR *waving his hand in anger*
Already he's become a Pole... my Brother.

Final Scene

The Campus Martius. KORDIAN is visible in the distance before a
platoon of soldiers. The crowd is talking in the foreground.

FIRST PERSON
Oh, look! The executioner is breaking
His sword over his head... [161]

---

160. The exercise field for the army. The name literally means "Field of Mars." It was the name given in ancient Rome for the military parade grounds, since Mars was the Roman god of war.
161. Done to a convicted officer as a sign of degradation.

SECOND PERSON
                              And did he scream?
I heard a scream.

FIRST PERSON
                    Oh, no, his lips are pale
He didn't say a word—but when the sword
Was broken on his head, an old man fainted
With a groan... Could it have been his old servant?

SECOND PERSON
They've taken his nobility away...

FIRST PERSON
It's been decreed that, as a peasant, he
Will never push a plow, instead-the plow
Will dig for him...

SECOND PERSON
                    They're giving him a blindfold
He refused it...

FIRST PERSON
                    An officer goes up...
He will begin... Oh, how my heart is beating!
They raise their weapons to their eyes...

SHOUTS FROM THE CROWD
                                        No! Stop!
The Adjutant...

FIRST PERSON
                    The officer can't see him...
He's raised his hand into the air...

End of Part One.

APPENDIX 1: CHARACTERS

ARCHANGEL—not specified, but is likely to represent the Archangel Michael, who is the emblem of the Ukraine, which was largely part of the Polish Commonwealth before the partitions.

ASHTORETH—One of the devils, originally the name of a Syrian moon goddess and probably derived from the Assyrian goddess of love and war, Astarte.

CADET—Kordian in disguise.

CARETAKER—A man who rents chairs at St. James Park in London.

CHAIRMAN—Patterned after Julian Ursyn Niemcewicz, poet and memoirist who fought with Kościuszko in his insurrection, was arrested with him, and accompanied Kościuszko on his triumphal trip to America. Niemcewicz was a guest of George Washington for a short time and then settled in New Jersey taking an American wife. He returned to Poland in 1802.

CREATURE—Represents the historian, Joachim Lelewel (1786-1861), accused in émigré circles of dampening the enthusiasm of the young insurgents and taking an indecisive stance on the dethroning of Nicholas I.

CZAR—Nicholas I, Czar of Russia. He also held the title of King of Poland, and as such was sworn in in 1829.

DOCTOR—The devil in disguise.

FIRST PERSON OF THE PROLOGUE—seems to represent Adam Mickiewicz, whose *Forefathers' Eve, part III*, presents the hero Konrad. *Kordian* is in many ways Słowacki's answer to that play, as discussed in the Introduction.

GEHENNA—Used as a name for a devil. The name is sometimes used for Hell itself, just as Hades was used by the Greeks to signify the god of the underworld and the underworld itself.

Kordian

GRAND DUKE—Constantine, the elder brother of Nicholas, who let himself be bypassed for the throne after the death of their elder brother Alexander. Constantine became regent of Poland, was married to a Polish noblewoman, and sought a certain independence in that role.

GRZEGORZ—Kordian's old, faithful servant, a former legionnaire who fought with Napoleon.

IMAGINATION—Personification of Kordian's emotion. *See* TERROR.

KORDIAN—Our hero. A young Polish nobleman.

TWARDOWSKI—The Polish Faust. His story runs parallel to the German version; however the Polish legend is more humorous and ends with Twardowski evading the devil by fleeing to the moon.

KURUTA—General Dmitri Kuruta, GRAND DUKE Constantine's Chief of Staff.

LAURA—Kordian's love interest. Her name recalls the love of Petrarch. It is never specifically mentioned, but it might be presumed that Kordian could not marry LAURA because of family objections (this would follow Słowacki's youthful experience). Although it is not clear that Kordian attempts suicide because of his love for LAURA, echoes of *The Sorrows of Young Werther* tend to suggest that.

MAID—A chambermaid at Kordian's manor.

MEPHISTOPHELES—The devil who tempts both Faust and Twardowski.

PARROT—According to the POPE, the PARROT houses the soul of Martin Luther.

PHANTOM—Unclear who the PHANTOM represents, but he makes references to two czars who killed their sons. Several Czars have been assassinated, but no king of Poland has ever been assassinated by a Pole.

POPE—In 1828 the POPE is Leo XII, however this POPE makes a reference to the Papal Encyclical of Gregory XVI, Leo's successor, so the character may be a kind of conflation of the two.

PRIEST—Although the PRIEST is not identified, he serves as an allusion to Father Piotr from Mickiewicz's *Forefathers' Eve*, who helps save Konrad from the devil's clutches.

SATAN—The leader of the Devils. He can be identified with Lucifer.

SECOND PERSON OF THE PROLOGUE—seems to represent a kind of anti-Mickiewicz.

SWISS GUARD—Traditional guard of the Vatican.

TERROR—Personification of Kordian's emotion, possibly a reference to the sons of Ares, the Greek god of war. *See IMAGINATION*.

THIRD PERSON OF THE PROLOGUE—could represent Słowacki himself, or more generally the spirit of art and the theater.

VIOLETTA—A beautiful Italian girl, interested in Kordian's money.

WITCH—Faithful servant of SATAN, at whose hut—formerly Twardowski's—SATAN holds his gathering of devils in preparation for the nineteenth century.

APPENDIX 2: TIMELINE

966
The establishment of the Polish state.

1385
Marriage of Queen Jadwiga to Władysław Jagiełło, establishing the dynastic union of Poland and Lithuania.

1569
The Union of Lublin, officially uniting Poland and Lithuania as the Commonwealth of Two Nations.

1683
King Jan Sobieski lifts the Turkish siege of Vienna.

1771
First partition of Poland.

1791
May 3 Constitution adopted.

1793
Second partition of Poland.

1794
Kościuszko Insurrection.

1795
Third partition; Poland disappears from the map of Europe until 1918.

1797
Formation of the Polish Legions in Italy (to fight with Napoleon).

1807
Establishment of the Grand Duchy of Warsaw.

1815
Dissolution of the Grand Duchy of Warsaw at the Congress of Vienna.

1830
November Insurrection.

BOOKS BY THE GREEN LANTERN PRESS

Forgery by **Amira Hanafi**, printed in an edition of 500 w/ silkscreen covers by Aay Preston-Mynt 2010 $20

The Mutation of Fortune by **Erica Adams**, printed in an edition of 500 w/ silkscreen covers by Aay Preston-Mynt 2010 $20

Fiction at Work, a collection of flash fiction from multiple authors, edited by Tobias Amadon Benglesdorf printed in an edition of 250 $10

The Concrete of Tight Places by **Justin Andrews**, printed in an edition of 500 w/ silkscreened covers by Nadine Nakanishi of Sonnenzimmer 2009 $20

CLOPS. by **Devin King**, printed in an edition of 250 w/ color plates by artist Brian McNearney 2009 $10

A Season In Hell by **Arthur Rimbaud**, translated by Nick Sarno printed in an edition of 500 w/ silkscreen covers by Nadine Nakanishi of Sonnenzimmer 2009 $20

So Much Better by **Terri Griffith**, nominated for the 2009 Lambda Literary prize, printed in an edition of 500 w/original artwork supplied by Zoe Crosher and silkscreen covers by Nick Butcher of Sonnenzimmer 2009 $20

Love Is Like A Certain Flower by **Stephanie Brooks**, printed in an edition of 250 w/ color plates supplied by the artist. 2009 $10

Fascia by **Ashley Murray**, a collection of short stories printed in an edition of 500 w/ silkscreen covers by Nadine Nakanishi of Sonnenzimmer 2009 $20

The North Georgia Gazette, a reprint of an original 1821 newspaper with excerpts from Captain Parry's log, an essay by John Huston & end notes by transcriber/poet Lily Robert-Foley printed in an edition of 250 w/ silkscreen covers & limited edition 7" record provided by Nick Butcher of Sonnenzimmer 2009 $30

Lust & Cashmere by A.E. Simns, winner of the 2008 IPPY Independent Voice award printed in an edition of 500 with silk screen covers by Alana Bailey 2007 $20

Fragments by David Carl, printed in an edition of 500 with silk screen covers by Alana Bailey 2008 $20

Talking With Your Mouth Full with essays by Lori Waxman, Claire Pentecost & Carrie Lambert-Beattie printed in an edition of 250 2008 $10

God Bless The Squirrel Cage by Nick Sarno, printed in an edition of 500 w/ silkscreen covers by Mat Daly 2006 $20

Urbesque by Moshe Zvi, a collection of short stories. Marvit printed in an edition of 500 w/ silkscreen covers by Mat Daly 2006 $20

Arts Administrator's Sketchbook edited by Elizabeth Chodos & Kerry Schneider, printed in an edition of 500 w/ silkscreen covers by Mat Daly 2007 $20

BOOKS PUBLISHED WITH THREEWALLS

Artists Run Chicago, printed in an edition of 500, 2009 $20

Paper & Carriage vols. 1, 2 & 3, a limited edition publication with silkscreen covers by Dan MacAdam of Crosshair, Sean Stuckey and Dan Wang. Published with threewalls $18/ea. Vol 1 nominated for the Utne Reader Award, Best New Publication 2008.

Phonebook 2007/2008, an annual index of alternative art spaces edited by Shannon Stratton & Caroline Picard $10

Phonebook 2008/2009, an annual index of alternative art spaces edited by Shannon Stratton & Caroline Picard $15

Gerard T. Kapolka received his Ph.D. in Polish Literature from the University of Chicago in 1981. He has taught at Rhode Island College, St. Mary's College in Orchard Lake, Michigan, Wagner College, and Rutgers University. Since 1995 he has been teaching at Santa Catalina School in Monterey, California ,where he is currently the Dean of Academics. His other translations include Stanislaw Wyspianski's *The Wedding* (Ardis, 1990) and Ignacy Krasicki's *Polish Fables* (Hippocrene, 1998).

Aay Preston-Myint is an artist and educator working in Chicago. He has been designing screen prints for posters, books, textiles, and two- and three-dimensional works since 1999, most recently under the imprint Dirt Rainbow. *www.dirtrainbow.net*

Dakota Brown works with and thinks about type. He studied graphic design at North Carolina State University and visual and critical studies at the School of the Art Institute of Chicago.

The Green Lantern Press is a non-profit paperback press determined to publish and distribute emerging and/or forgotten works in conjunction with the activities of Green Lantern Gallery and Lantern Projects. Dedicated to the "slow media" approach, each work is printed in small collector's editions. This is in keeping with a general attitude about consumerism and the material we print, namely that we only make what will be used, just as all that we make is of fine quality and innovative character.

Committed to forming alternative and sustainable models for the distribution and presentation of noncommercial contemporary art, the nonprofit Press and Gallery is partnered with a for-profit Bookstore and Performance Space in order to explore different possibilities to support artists, writers and community. We celebrate the integration of artistic mediums. We celebrate the amateur, the idealist and those who recognize the importance of small independent practice.

Ultimately, we hope to build a community of collectors who support us because they believe in our product and wish to sustain the relationships we foster between burgeoning or marginalized authors and the public.